DESCRIPTIONS OF LORD COBHAM'S GARDENS AT STOWE (1700 – 1750)

DESCRIPTIONS OF
LORD COBHAM'S GARDENS
AT STOWE
(1700 – 1750)

Edited by
G.B. CLARKE

BUCKINGHAMSHIRE RECORD SOCIETY

No. 26

MCMXC

ISBN 0 901198 25 0 Cloth bound edition
ISBN 0 901198 26 9 Paper bound edition

Designed and Typeset
in ITC New Baskerville
by R. Euan Williams
5 Arbutus Close
Dorchester, Dorset

and printed by Henry Ling Ltd
The Dorset Press
Dorchester, Dorset
on Glastonbury Book Antique Laid
and Parilux Matt Cream

CONTENTS

Introduction

No gardens in eighteenth-century England were more famous than those at Stowe in Buckinghamshire. They were more frequently visited, more influential and more often described than any others outside London, becoming the subject of a growing stream of journals, poems and guidebooks throughout the century. The aim of the present volume is to collect into one place the most important pieces written on Stowe between 1700 and 1750, so as to throw new light on the development of the gardens and reflect the changing attitude of informed opinion towards them. The dates beginning and ending the period coincide almost exactly with those of Lord Cobham's long reign. In 1700 he had been in possession for a little over two years; in 1750 he had just died, and Richard Grenville, his nephew and successor, was taking the management of the estate into his own hands. In practice, the collection starts in 1724, when Cobham's gardening activities first gained Stowe a national reputation.

A surprising fact which emerges is that very few friends of the family recorded anything interesting about the gardens. Perhaps, like most of us, they took familiar things for granted. Henrietta Louisa, Countess of Pomfret, who lived at Easton Neston, may be cited as an example. She was an intelligent, well-educated woman, with cultural and antiquarian tastes, a near neighbour, who mentioned visiting Stowe at least three times in her diary. But though she twice recorded that she was shown round by her hosts, she said little more about the gardens than that they had increased in size since her last visit and were extremely fine. The same is true of other friends of the family. The correspondence of Lady Denbigh and Lady Suffolk, and even of Alexander Pope, all of whom regularly visited Stowe, provides almost nothing of substance. Gilbert West, one of Cobham's "mob of nephews" and author of the descriptive poem *Stowe*, is a notable exception, but apart from him the useful information comes from outsiders.

The most often quoted of these, Horace Walpole, recorded his first comments in a letter to George Montagu of July 1751, just too late for inclusion in this volume. "I ran through the gardens at Stowe, which I have seen before," he wrote, "and had only time to be charmed with the variety of scenes. I do like that Albano glut of buildings, let them be ever so much condemned." Vivid remarks like this capture the imagination of the reader, and quoting them enlivens a dull paragraph. But Walpole's very qualities as a letter writer make him a dubious witness. The trouble is that he is just as interested in how his audience will respond as he is in the subject of his letter. So he is prepared to select, exaggerate and distort the evidence for the sake of effect. No one who enjoys lively writing could bring himself to discard Walpole's descriptions, but for reliable witnesses the historian has to turn to more literal commentators.

Fortunately they existed, and some of their descriptions survive. They reveal themselves in all their human frailty, dedicated enthusiasts who walked

round the gardens with an earnestness which at times is comic: people like
Jeremiah Milles, who was determined to copy down all the Latin inscriptions
in Nelson's Seat, but must have written them out on too cramped a piece of
paper and got them muddled up; or the visitor of 1742, who methodically
drew a plan of the gardens, squaring it off neatly, but missed the sweeping
diagonals which governed Bridgeman's lay-out; or Sir Roger and Lady
Newdigate, one of whom took the measurements of the Chinese House,
while the other wrote down the figures in a notebook. It is on the evidence
of people like these, of transparent, fallible honesty, that a jury would acquit
or convict. Walpole's testimony would be dismissed as too clever by half.

The poets added prestige to Lord Cobham's gardens. The extracts from
longer poems by Pope and Thomson have been quoted before, but they
each contain some of the finest lines ever written about Stowe. Congreve's
verse epistle to Cobham has been unduly neglected; West's topographical
poem on his uncle's gardens is among the best things of its kind; and
Boyse's pedestrian verse, though scarcely deserving to be printed in the
same company, is an interesting work of its date and easier to read here than
by instalments in the yellowing pages of the *Gentleman's Magazine*.

The reprinted prose works include the three earliest published guides
to Stowe: part of the Appendix to the 1742 edition of Defoe's *Tour*; the
1744 edition of Seeley's *Description of the Gardens*, the first guidebook; and
Les Charmes de Stow, in effect the first guidebook in French, whose origins
are a mystery. Had space allowed, Gilpin's *Dialogue upon the Gardens* would
have been included. This was not possible, but fortunately it is accessible in
reprinted editions elsewhere.

The Development of the Gardens (1700 – 1750)

When Sir Richard Temple, afterwards Viscount Cobham, inherited Stowe
from his father in 1697, he took over a house and gardens which were less
than twenty years old. The house was a handsome brick building with stone
quoins, completed in 1683. The formal gardens lay southwards in three
terraces, as far as a lane which slanted across the vista (Fig. 1). To the east
was the mediaeval parish church, to the west a walled kitchen garden, and
beyond that a semi-circular area laid out as a wilderness. Below the lane an
avenue of poplars continued the central axis of the lay-out as far as the
stream. These were the gardens which Celia Fiennes described in about 1694
as "one below another with low breast walls and taress walkes,…replenished
with all the curiosities or requisites for ornament pleasure and use."

Sir Richard Temple was a strong Whig and a distinguished officer in the
wars against Louis XIV. Dismissed by the Tories in 1713, he was restored to
his army command in the following year on the accession of George I, and
created Baron Cobham. His marriage in 1715 to Anne Halsey, an heiress,
with the restitution of his army pay as a general gave him real scope for
improvements; and when he was raised another step in the peerage to
Viscount Cobham in 1719, he embarked upon a further programme of

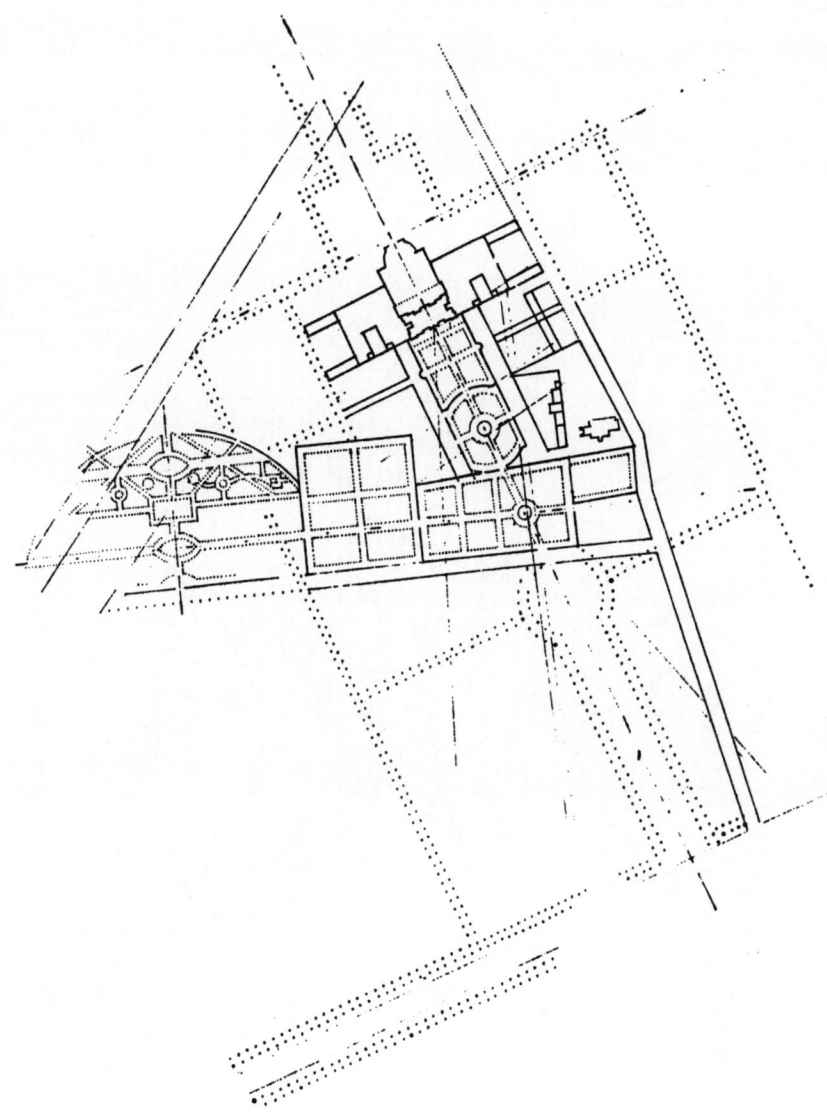

Fig.1 Stowe in 1700
from a reconstructed plan of the gardens by David Sumpster

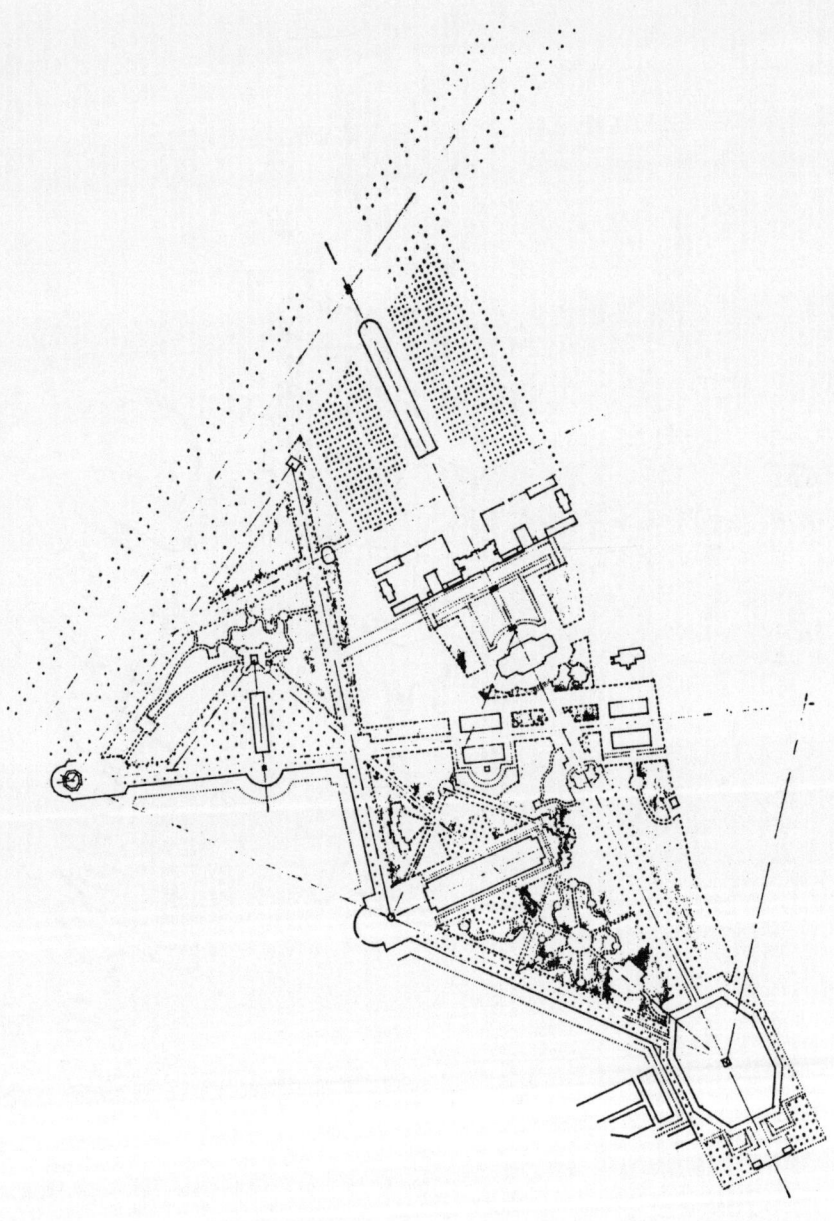

Fig.2 Stowe in 1724
from a reconstructed plan of the gardens by David Sumpster

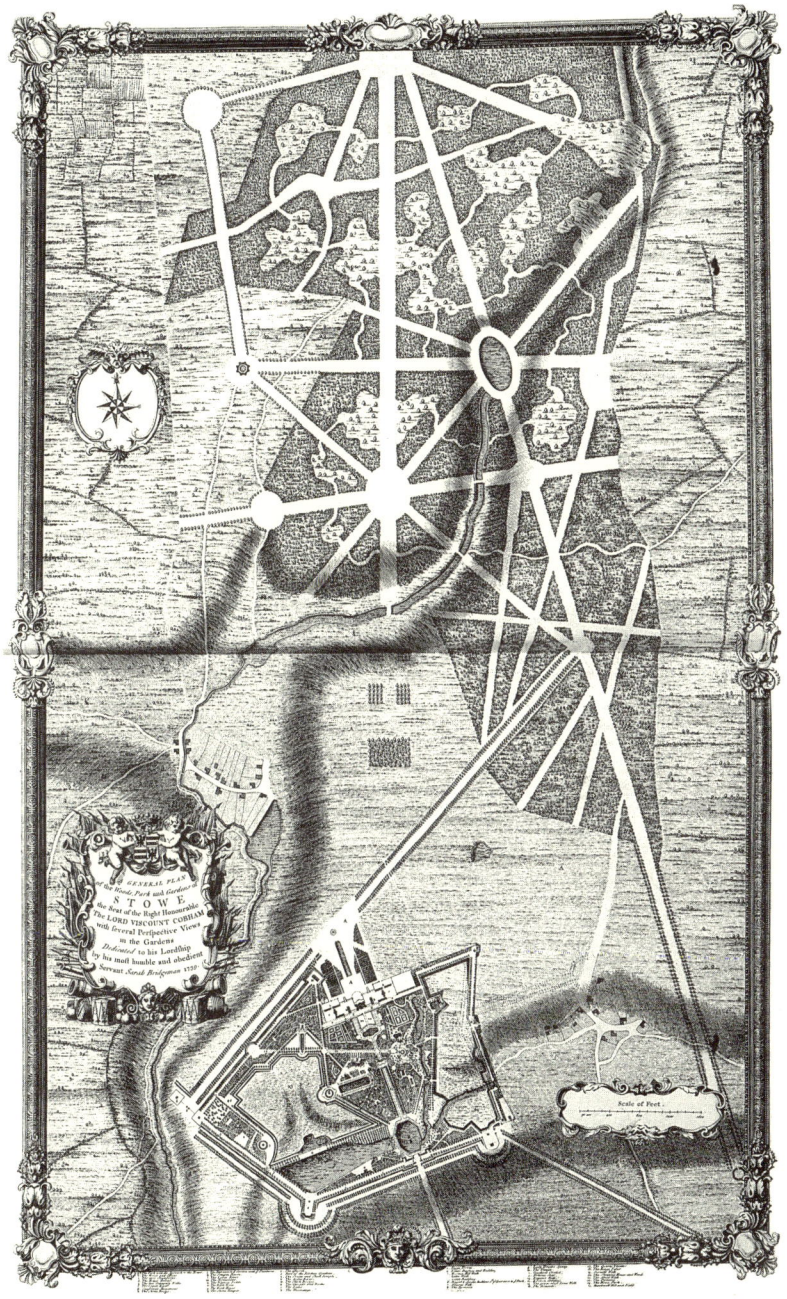

Fig.3
Plan of the park and gardens published by Sarah Bridgeman in 1739

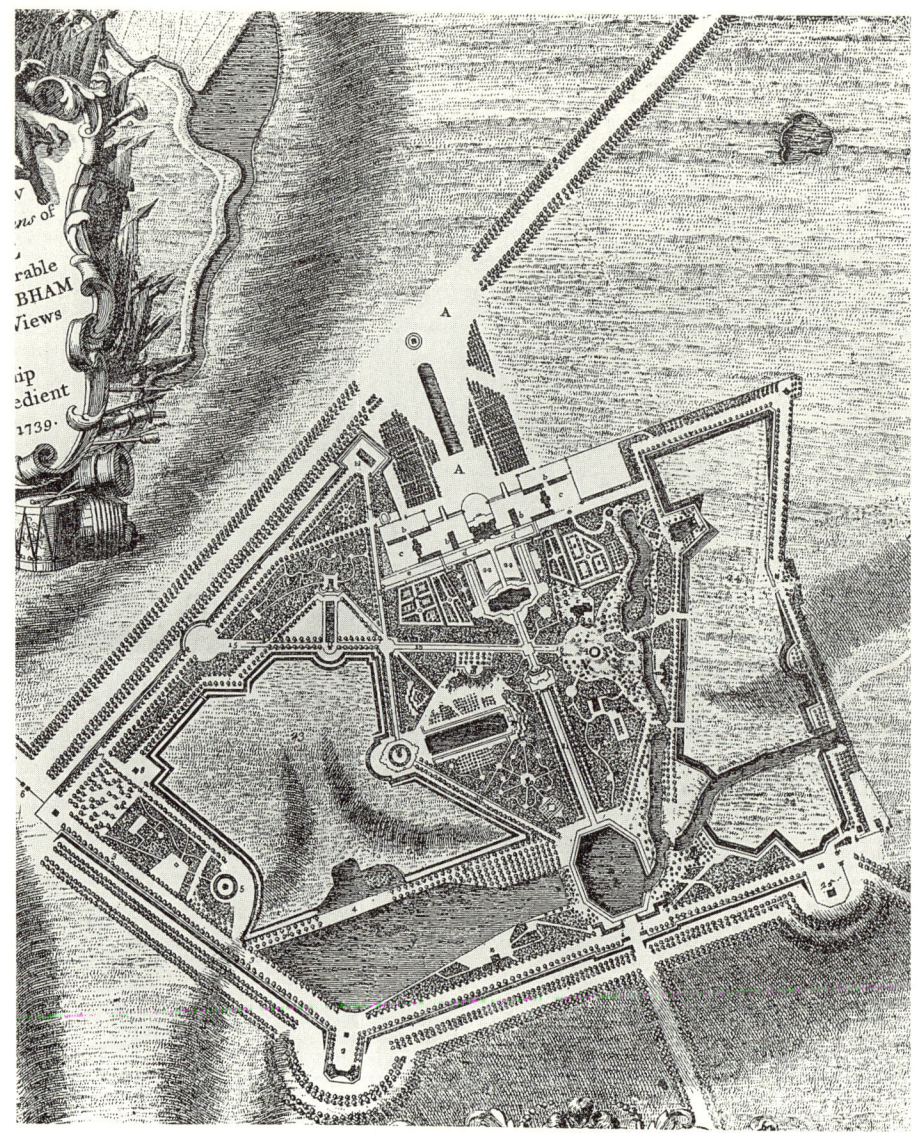

Fig.4
Detail of Sarah Bridgeman's 1739 Plan

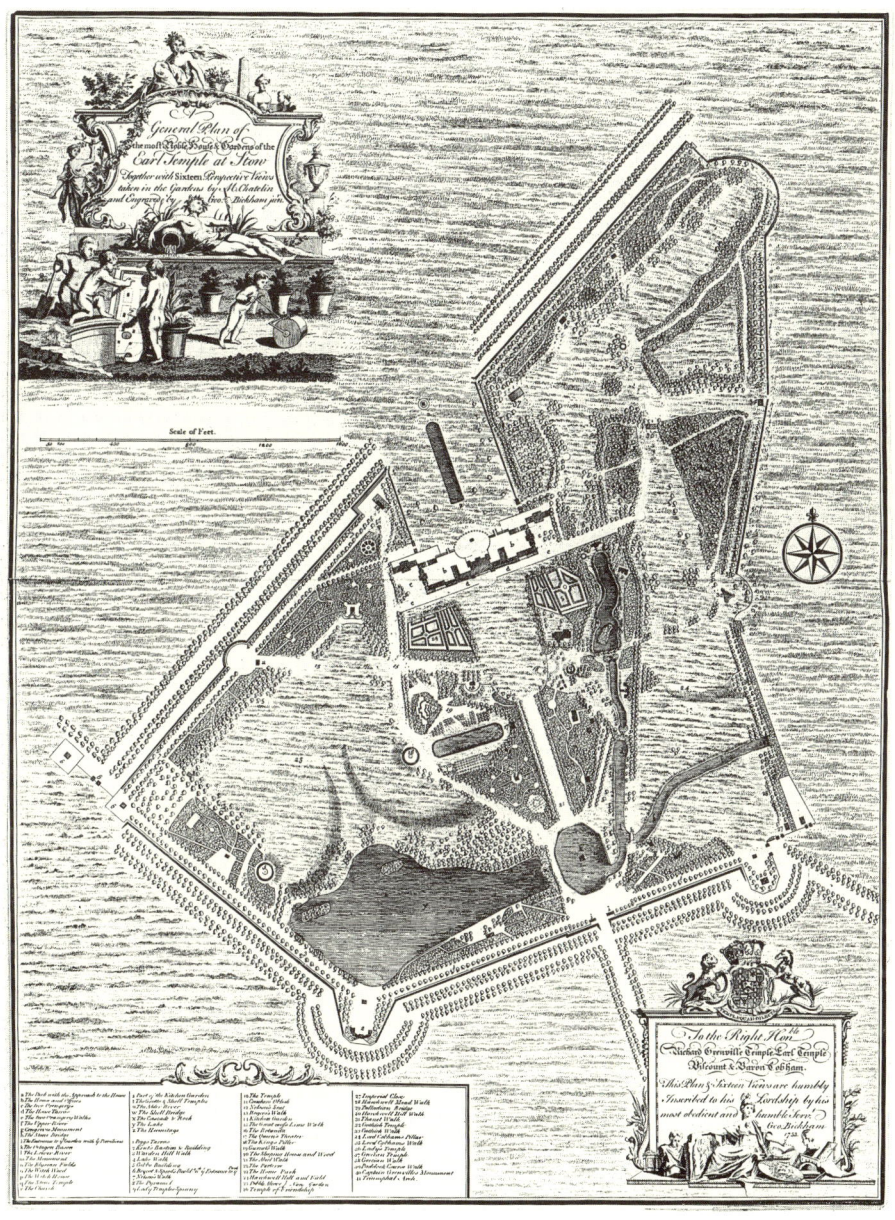

Fig.5
George Bickham's Plan of 1753

PLAN OF THE GARDENS AND KEY

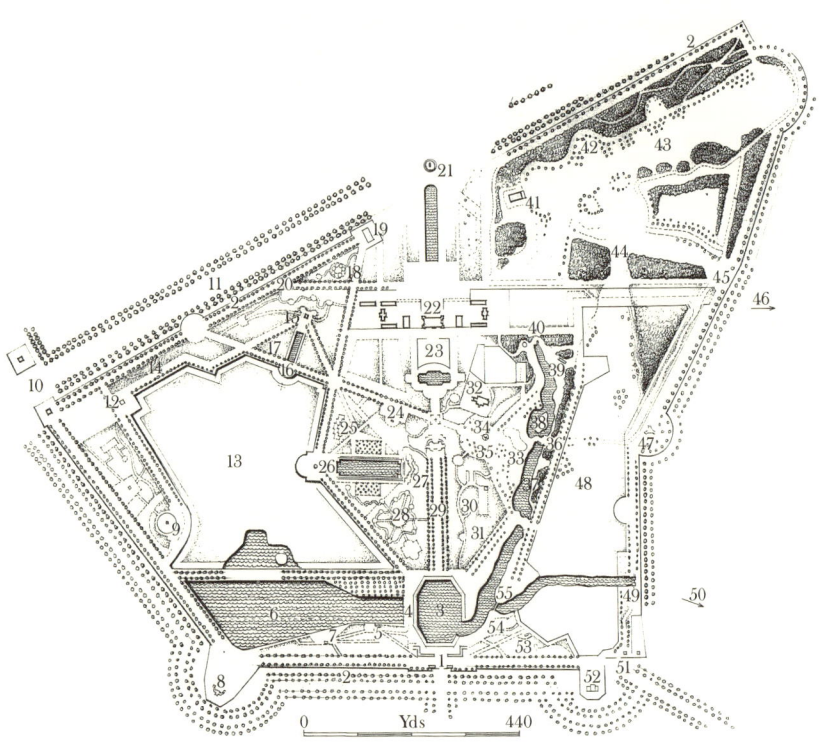

0 Yds 440

1. Lake Pavilions
2. Ha-ha
3. Octagon Basin & Guglio
4. Cascade
5. Cold Bath
6. Eleven-Acre Lake
7. Hermitage
8. Temple of Venus
9. Gibbs' Building or
   Belvidere
10. Boycott Pavilions
11. Course
12. Pyramid
13. Home Park
14. St. Augustine's Cave
15. Temple of Bacchus
16. Coucher's Obelisk
17. Great Cross Lime Walk
18. Saxon Deities
19. Nelson's Seat
20. Nelson's Walk
21. Statue of George I

22. Stowe House
23. Parterre (until 1742)
24. Statue of George II
25. Dido's Cave
26. Rotunda
27. Statue of Q. Caroline
28. Sleeping Parlour
29. Abele Walk
30. Witch House
31. Apollo and the Muses –
    the Spring of Helicon
    (after c. 1742)
32. Parish Church
33. Elysian Fields
34. Temple of Ancient
    Virtue
35. Temple of Modern
    Virtue
36. Shell Bridge
37. Temple of British
    Worthies
38. Chinese House

39. Temple of
    Contemplation
40. Grotto & Shell Temples
41. Grecian Temple (later
    Temple of Concord
    and Victory)
42. Captain Grenville's
    Monument
43. Grecian Valley
44. Lady's Temple
45. Lord Cobham's Pillar
46. Keeper's Lodge (later
    Bourbon Tower)
47. Gothic Temple
48. Hawkwell Field
49. Palladian Bridge
50. Stowe Castle
51. Imperial Closet
52. Temple of Friendship
53. Pebble Alcove
54. Congreve Monument
55. Stone Bridge

expansion which would turn the country gentleman's estate of his father into a princely mansion with a more than princely garden. Sir John Vanbrugh, an old friend from the Kit-Cat Club, was his architectural adviser, and Charles Bridgeman was engaged as garden designer. The sequence of his improvements can most simply be explained by a series of phases with approximate dates.

PHASE 1 (1715-19) A grander entrance court was created on the north side of the house, and alterations were made within the old gardens on the south, the three Caroline compartments being thrown into a single great parterre in the French style. Vanbrugh designed buildings to embellish the gardens.

PHASE 2 (1720-25) On Vanbrugh's and Bridgeman's recommendation the gardens were extended as far south as the stream, which was dammed to create the Octagon Pond. Since the approach road blocked eastward development, a salient was pushed out west into Home Park with the Rotunda at its head. Bridgeman's ha-ha provided a concealed boundary wall on the south and west sides of the lay-out (Fig. 2).

PHASE 3 (1726-32) The western side of the gardens was extended and completed. Home Park, an area of rough pasture, was brought within the gardens and surrounded by terraced walks. The stream was dammed a second time to create the Eleven-Acre Lake, and a new approach road was built right round the southern and western boundaries of the gardens to replace the old road to the east. After Vanbrugh's death in 1726, James Gibbs and then William Kent were engaged to design the buildings (Fig. 4).

In about 1733 forty acres were enclosed to the east of the old road and this area was then developed in two phases (Fig. 4).

PHASE 4 (1733-39) The little valley running south was laid out as the Elysian Fields. All the buildings in this area were by William Kent, and the style of the lay-out followed his idea of "beautiful nature". Cobham's quarrel with Sir Robert Walpole led to his joining the 'Patriot' Opposition and adding a political overtone to the philosophic programme of the gardens.

PHASE 5 (1739-43) Hawkwell Field was laid out in a style similar to *ferme ornée*, with stock free to graze right up to the walls of the buildings, all of which were designed by Gibbs. Meanwhile in front of the house the parterre was removed and grassed over, the first step to remodelling the old gardens. Lancelot ('Capability') Brown joined the staff as head gardener in 1741.

PHASE 6 (1743-49) A new area was enclosed to the north-east, and the Grecian Valley was laid out with a second vista diagonally east towards the Cobham Pillar. Between the axes of these two vistas a new walled garden was built, so that the old kitchen garden could be transferred and more space gained on the south side of the house (Fig. 5). But a dozen more years were to pass before Earl Temple threw open the whole southern vista.

Editorial Practice

The spelling, capital letters and punctuation of the manuscript extracts have been preserved except where they are positively misleading. A capital letter has always been inserted after a full stop, 'ye' has been changed to 'the' throughout, common abbreviations have been silently expanded, and many trivial errors have been put right without comment. Other editorial intervention has been kept to a minimum; where it occurs, it is indicated by square brackets.

The extracts from printed eighteenth-century books have been laid out in the same way as the originals. They are not facsimiles, but an attempt has been made to print them in a nearly identical style. The original pagination has been indicated in Seeley's *Description* and in *Les Charmes de Stow*, since these are two rare books which are thought never to have been reprinted before.

The text of the verse extracts follows that of standard modern editions, any changes being indicated in the notes. But the capital letters authorised by eighteenth-century editions have been retained.

Note on the Illustrations

All the illustrations have been taken from the three collections of Stowe engravings published between 1700 and 1750. The first, and incomparably the finest, is a set of fifteen views drawn by a Frenchman, Jacques Rigaud, in 1733 and engraved by himself and Bernard Baron. Commissioned by Charles Bridgeman, the garden designer, they were a commercial failure and were only published after his death by his widow Sarah in 1739, with a map of that date (Figs. 3 and 4). When she died, the remaining stock was bought up by a consortium of booksellers and was re-issued for binding, with a separate title page, in 1746. These engravings are much too large to be reproduced in the present volume, but some examples of details have been included.

The second collection is contained in the ten-page booklet of engraved views of the garden buildings which Benton Seeley published in 1750 as a supplement to his guidebook of a few years earlier. All of these engravings are reproduced on pages 148 to 157, where the headnote explains their provenance.

The third source is George Bickham, the London publisher and engraver, whose dubious publishing activities for the Stowe tourist market are related below (see page 174). There is more to be said in his favour as an illustrator. In 1753 he was to issue a set of sixteen views engraved by himself from views taken on the spot by J.-B. Châtelain. Though inferior to Rigaud's set, they are very informative, and they too were accompanied by a map (Fig.5). Three years earlier, in 1750, he had engraved thirty illustrations for his *Beauties of Stow*, a selection from which is reproduced in the following pages.

Acknowledgments

Acknowledgment is due to the owners of unpublished letters and journals who have given their permission for extracts to be printed, and to librarians and archivists who have made available material deposited in their care: to Lady Lucas and the Bedfordshire Record Office for Marchioness Grey's *Letterbook*; to Earl Cathcart for the 8th Lord Cathcart's *Diary*; to Viscount Daventry and the Warwickshire Record Office for Lady Newdigate's *Journal* and Sir Roger Newdigate's drawing of the Chinese House; to Professor Michael McCarthy for allowing me to use material from his forthcoming book on Sir Roger Newdigate; to the Trustees of the Will of Major Peter George Evelyn and Christ Church, Oxford, for Sir John Evelyn's *Journal*; to Mrs. Anna Larcombe (née Knight) for Thomas Knight's *Journal*; to Simon Houfe, Esq., for *Les Charmes de Stow*; to the Director and Trustees of the Huntington Library, California, for *Lord Cobhams Gardens 1738*; to the Council of the Yorkshire Archaeological Society for Edward Southwell's *Journal*; to the British Library for Lord Perceval's *Letter to Daniel Dering*, George Grenville's *Letter to Richard Grenville*, Anne Grenville's *Letter to Richard Grenville*, George Vertue's *Notebooks*, *The Journal of John Dodd's Tour*, Jeremiah Milles' *Diary*, and the anonymous *Tour* of 1742; to English Heritage for allowing me to use David Sumpster's reconstructed drawings of the lay-out; to Christopher Chaplin for preparing the numbered key to the gardens; to the Headmaster of Stowe School for giving me the freedom of the Stowe Collection. I am grateful to all these people and organisations for their kind assistance.

I would like to record my appreciation for the encouragement and support I have received from Dr. Eileen Scarff, General Editor of the Buckinghamshire Record Society, and from Hugh Hanley, the Secretary of the Society, throughout the preparation of this volume.

Lastly, I owe an immeasurable debt of gratitude to the friends living and dead, too numerous to mention by name, who have shared their knowledge of Stowe over many years, generously passing on the descriptions of the gardens which they have discovered in the course of their researches.

George Clarke
February 1990

John, Viscount Perceval,
afterwards 1st Earl Egmont (1683 – 1748)

It is lucky that the earliest visitor to Lord Cobham's gardens whose detailed observations survive should have been so perceptive a critic. For Lord Perceval went to Stowe in the summer of 1724 just as the garden extension proposed by Vanbrugh and Bridgeman in 1719 was reaching completion, and his reactions, coming from a knowledgeable aristocratic tourist, are extremely valuable.

John Perceval, created Earl of Egmont in 1733, was at this time still Viscount Perceval in the peerage of Ireland. Born near Cork, he was educated at Westminster School and Magdalen College, Oxford, and in 1702 was elected a fellow of the Royal Society. He spent the years 1705 to 1707 abroad on the Grand Tour, before taking a seat in the Irish House of Commons. Later, in 1727, he became M.P. for Harwich at Westminster.

From 1729 he was closely associated with General Oglethorpe's scheme to found a new colony (Georgia) in America for insolvent debtors and fugitives from religious persecution, devoting much of his time, money and influence to this cause. His opponents ridiculed him for his pomposity and fanaticism, and parts of his Stowe description do perhaps seem a trifle over-enthusiastic—much of the planting in the new extension to the garden, for example, can have been little more than a year old. But he was a well-informed man, with interests in a wide variety of subjects, and he had an able mind. When he contrasted the *irregularity* of the whole design at Stowe with the *regularity* of the parts, he put his finger on the essential character of Bridgeman's lay-out, and his comments on the aesthetic effect of the ha-ha are equally acute.

Lord Perceval and his wife, who were making a short summer tour, had already visited, among other places, Hall Barn, Shotover, the city and university of Oxford, and Blenheim. They looked round Stowe on Thursday, August 13th, after spending an uncomfortable night at the New Inn, the first but by no means the last visitors to complain about its wretched accommodation. This letter was written from Brackley to a relative, Daniel Dering, on the following day. It is here printed complete, except for details of Lady Perceval's health.

from *Letter to Daniel Dering, 14 August 1724*

fryday night 7 a'clock

Dear Daniel,

In my last I told you the good Stomach my wife had at Stow my Ld Cobham's Inn, and gave you a journal of her health till Wednesday night. Our Inn was a scurvy one and had not beds for all. Those of us who went to bed could not sleep for fleas and gnats, however my wife had no cholick...

Now for our journey. Yesterday we saw my Ld Cobhams house, which within these 5 years, has gained the reputation of being the finest seat in England, and well deserved our going so far out of the way to see. The house is of brick and 13 windows in front, with a considerable depth. Old Sir Richard built it, but this Lord his son, new furnished and much embellish'd it. The tapestry was made at Brussels, and next to that in the Town house of Brussels is the finest I have seen. It represents the duty of the horse in Campaign. The rooms are all on a line, and adornished with some good paintings, particularly a large chimney piece by Rembrant of a soldier menacing a man in prison. Before the house is a large Court, at the entrance of which stands an Equestral Statue of K. George, and to this Court is an Avenue lately planted.

The Gardens, by reason of the good contrivance of the walks, seem to be three times as large as they are. They contain but 28 acres, yet took us up two hours. It is entirely new, and tho' begun but eleven years ago is now almost finished. From the lower end you ascend a multitude of steps (but at several distances) to the Parterre, and from thence several more to the house, which standing high comands a fine prospect. One way they can see 26 miles. It is impossible to give you an exact Idea of this garden, but we shall shortly have a graving of it. It consists of a great number of walks, terminated by Summer houses and heathen temples of different structure, and adorned with statues cast from the Anticks. Here you see the Temple of Apollo, there a Triumphal Arch. The garden of Venus is delightfull; you see her standing in her Temple at the head of a noble bason of water, and opposite to her an Amphitheater, with statues of Gods and Godesses; this bason is sorounded with walks and groves, and overlook'd from a considerable heigth by a tall Column of the Composite Order, on which stands the statue of Pr. George in his Robes. At the end of the gravel walk leading from the house are two heathen Temples with a circle of water 2 acres and a quarter large, in the midst whereof is a Gulio or pyramid, at least 50 foot high, from the top of which it is designed that water shall fall, being by pipes convey'd thro' the heart of it. Half way up this walk is another fine bason with a pyramid in it 30 foot high, and nearer the house you meet a fountain that plays 40 foot. The Cross walks end in Vistos, arches and statues, and the private ones cut thro' groves are delightfull. You think twenty times you have no more to see, and of a sudden find yourself in some new garden or walk as finish'd and adorn'd as that you left. Nothing is more irregular in the whole, nothing more regular in the parts, which totally differ one from the other. This shews my Lords good tast, and his fondness to the place appears by the great expence he has been at. We all know how chargeable it is to make a garden with tast; to make one of a sudden is more so; but to erect so many Summer houses, Temples, Pillars, Piramids and Statues, most of fine hewn stone, the rest of guilded lead, would drain the richest purse, and I doubt not but much of his wifes great fortune has been sunk in it. The Pyramid at the End of one of the walks is a copy in mignature of the most famous one in Egypt, and the only thing of the kind I think in England. Bridgman laid out the ground and plan'd the whole which cannot fail of recomending him to business.[1] What adds to the bewty of this garden is, that it is not bounded by Walls, but by a Ha-hah, which leaves you the sight of a bewtifull woody Country, and makes you ignorant how far the high planted walks extend.

[1] *[Added later in the margin]* Mr Bridgman was afterwards made the Kings Ch. Gardiner.

(BL Add. MS 47030, ff. 156-9)

Detail of engraving by Jacques Rigaud
View from the foot of the Pyramid

Anonymous
probably Edward Southwell

A second visitor in 1724 was the anonymous writer of a manuscript in the collection of the Yorkshire Archaeological Society. He toured the garden in the same week as Lord Perceval—on the previous Sunday, August 9th—and his brief description, like the two which follow, complements Perceval's conveniently. His only identified error was to describe Vanbrugh's Lake Pavilions (line 9) as Ionic, when they were actually Doric.

This blunder is understandable, since the tour was no weekend ramble, with time to take notes and savour experiences at leisure, but a marathon lasting several weeks, when two, even three, country houses or gardens were visited in a single day. Starting from London on August 6th, they reached Stowe on day three, having already made exhaustive inspections of Cannons, Moor Park and Tring. The author, whose dates are not known, is thought to have been Edward Southwell, and his companion, named in the text as "my Cousin W. Knatchbull", was almost certainly Wyndham Knatchbull of Mersham-le-Hatch in Kent.

Nearly five weeks and more than sixty country houses later they reached their destination at York. We should be thankful that Stowe came so early in their Grand Tour of England.

from *Account of my Journey begun 6 Aug 1724*

From Buckingham we went 2 miles to Lord Cobhams at Stowe, where he has an house of 13 windows in front, with offices at both ends built by Sir John Vanbrugh. There are 28 acres of Gardening all in a descent from the House: to which there is a Terrass then a descent of 3 parterres, next a long Avenue of a double row of Abeals at the end of which is an Octogonal Pond of 400 feet by 300 ft with an Obelisque 60 feet high in the middle which has a fine Terrass with two Seats and 2 Colonnades of Ionic Pillars to front it, and which is in the Center of the House, and of a Rotundo also Ionic Pillars and a gilt Statue of Venus in the midst, as also of a Corinthian fluted Column 40 feet high, with a Statue of the Prince of Wales, which cost £80, in Stone and is $7\frac{1}{2}$ feet high at Top. The Rotundo fronts a fine Canal and Amphitheatre of Slopes and Statues. There are also 2 Seats adorn'd with Ionic pillars, which front several long Gravel walks. The main Parterre is surrounded with an Amphitheatre of Ewe Niches, with the Muses etc between them.

The Prospect of the Country, and My Lord['s] fine woods of 10 miles in length and 2 miles in breadth were worth observing, through which we pass'd and dined at Mr Kingstons at the White Horse in Towcester.

(Yorkshire Archaeological Society, MS 328, ff. 5-6)

Sir John Evelyn (1682 – 1763)

Sir John Evelyn, Bart., grandson of the diarist, who was travelling from his family home at Wotton, Surrey, to Oxford in May 1725, stopped to look at places of interest on the way, arriving at Stowe on May 17th, rather earlier in the year than most visitors. The party included his son.

Cobham, like several of Marlborough's other senior generals, had commissioned a set of Brussels tapestries based on "The Art of War" by De Hondt to hang in his house. The subjects of the various scenes were conventional and general, but clearly the legend was already being fostered at Stowe that one of the pieces represented a particular incident in the Flanders campaigns in which Cobham himself was involved. Blaregnies is a mile or two north-east of Malplaquet.

After visiting Blenheim later on the same day, Evelyn and his party spent the night at Woodstock. On May 18th they called at Ditchley, then being built, and were in Oxford by one o'clock. There they were found by a Fellow of Queen's, who took them to the college, where "my Son enter'd his name in the Buttery book". Afterwards they visited the library and attended prayers in the college chapel, specially admiring Thornhill's window over the altar.

from his *Journal (1725)*

May 17.   Reached Buckingham about half an hour after nine. Having visited the Church which has a good tower, and seen the ruins of above 100 houses destroy'd lately by fire, we went to Lord Cobhams at Stowe 2 miles further, where the gardens are very noble, and adorn'd with Temples, one being a Rotunda with a gilt statue of the Venus of Medici in the midle, Statues, Obelisks, Pillars, and Porticos, and consisting of 30 acres, in the keeping of which 12 men, 2 women and 8 boys are employ'd. There being no walls to be seen, the prospect of the Country is very extensive—from the garden, as well as from the House, which is large and good tho' built by Sir Richard Temple his father some years since. In one of the rooms below are hangings representing the battle of Blaregnies in the wood near Mons, in which Lord Cobham was, [being] fought 31 Augt 1709.

We proceeded by Midleton Stoney an hunting seat of the late Lord Carleton...

(Christ Church, Oxford, Evelyn MS 248C, ff. 14-15)

Anonymous
probably Thomas Knight (c.1701 – 1781)

Thomas Knight was born Thomas Brodnax, but he changed his name by Act of Parliament first to May and then to Knight, when two wealthy maternal relatives in turn made him their heir. He entered Balliol College, Oxford, in 1720, succeeded his father in 1726, and inherited the May estate in the same year. So in 1727 he was his own master with a considerable independent fortune.

His tour of England was more extensive than any of the three already mentioned. Starting from London on June 8th, he travelled as far north as Newcastle, then south-west to Bath, and from there back to London, which he reached on September 23rd. According to his own reckoning the total distance was 1,164 miles.

The entries in his journal are brief, little more than notes, but he usefully confirms several details of the garden's development, and his comments on travelling conditions are interesting. It is not surprising that the White Horse at Towcester was among the better inns of the day, since Watling Street was then one of the busiest roads in central England.

from his *Journal*

June 10th 1727

From Ailsbury to Whitchurch 3 Miles. From Whitchurch to Winslow 3 Miles, very bad Road. From Winslow to Buckingham 6 Miles. Buckingham Town was burn't down in 1724 but is now rebuilt. From Buckingham to Stow 2 Miles. From Stow to Tocester 6 Miles, a deep bad Road. Northamptonshire. At Tocester, the White Horse, a very good Inn.

This part of Buckinghamshire is an open Country, upon a deep Clay soil, good for Corn. The Roads deep and bad. The poor people are cheifly employ'd in making narrow Lace.

Stow, Lord Cobham's

A handsome Avenue above half a Mile, with Abeal Trees on each side. An Octagon Bason at the Bottom of the Gardens, with an obelisque in it. The House Brick with 13 Windows Front. The Gardens very well laid out in Wood walls, 28 Acres. A Rotunda. A Statue of K. George on Horseback. A Statue of P. George on a Single Column. A Statue of the Princess on 4 Columns. A Rotunda with a Venus de Medicis gilt. The Park 400 Acres.

(Private collection of Mrs. Anna Larcombe)

William Congreve (1670 – 1729)

By 1728 Stowe was firmly established on the tourist circuit. The extension of the garden westward beyond the Rotunda, to include Home Park and the Eleven-Acre Lake, was taking shape, and Cobham's gardening ambitions could be regarded as almost fulfilled. For other reasons too a slowing down in the pace of his life was to be expected. Many of his associates were now dead, including his former chief Marlborough, the warrior-king George I, and his old friend Sir John Vanbrugh, on whom he had relied so long for architectural advice. Cobham himself was in his mid-fifties and nearing the age for retirement from public affairs. It is in this context that Congreve's poem should be read.

Congreve was five years older than Cobham. Like Vanbrugh, he too was a dining crony from the days of the Kit-Cat Club, and he had known Stowe, in and out of season, for many years. Snowed up there one New Year's Day, probably in 1714, he wrote to friends in London: "God knows when the snow will let me stirr; or if a thaw should come upon it when the flouds will be down. I am by a great fire yet my ink freezes so fast I cannot write. The Hautboys who playd to us last night had their breath froze in their instruments till it dropt of the ends of them in icicles." After his death he was not forgotten by Cobham, who was one of the pall-bearers at his funeral and who erected a monument in 1736 to his friend's memory. A statue, designed by William Kent, portrays a monkey gazing at its own reflection in a mirror, a witty variation of traditional ape-lore which can still be seen on an island in the Octagon Lake.

Two of Congreve's poems had already been addressed to Cobham, an epistle ('Of Pleasing') and a tale ('An Impossible Thing'), both lively pieces but neither of much consequence. This second verse epistle, however, is an altogether finer poem, worthy to stand beside Pope's compositions of the same kind. Congreve writes as one who has "retired without regret" and asks if the time has not come when his friend Cobham should follow him, to view the ways of the world with philosophic detachment.

In fact, of course, the poem is an ironic reminder to us that in 1728 Cobham's most influential period of activity had not yet begun. His busiest involvement in national politics and his greatest innovations at Stowe, which were to change the direction of English gardening, took place in the 1730s and 1740s, when Cobham was already sixty and most men of his age would have left the main action. The restless energy of this man in his sixties and seventies was remarkable.

The poem was first published by Lewis in 1729. The pre-publication version printed here was included in a letter of 19 March 1729 from George Grenville to his brother Richard, later Earl Temple, then on his Grand Tour. According to George, the original had been "sent to my Ld Cobham in a letter from Bath 24 August 1728".

Of Improving the Present Time
(1728)

Sincerest Critic of my Prose or Rhyme,
Tell how thy pleasing Stowe employs thy Time.
Say, Cobham, what amuses thy Retreat,
Or Schemes of War, or Stratagems of State?
Dost thou recall to Mind with Joy or Grief
Great Marlborough's Actions, that immortal Chief,
Whose slightest Trophy raised in each Campaign
More than sufficed to signalise a Reign?
Does the Remembrance, rising, warm thy Heart
With Glory past, where Thou thyself hadst Part,   10
Or dost thou grieve indignant, now, to see
The fruitless End of all that Victory?
To see the Audacious Foe, so late subdued,
Dispute those Terms for which so long they sued,
As if Britannia now were sunk so low,
To beg that Peace she wonted to bestow.
Be far that Guilt, be never known such Shame,
That England should retract her rightful Claim,
Or, ceasing to be dreaded and adored,
Stain with the Pen the Lustre of her Sword!   20
Or dost thou give the Winds afar to blow
Each vexing Thought and Heart-devouring Woe,

And fix thy Mind alone on rural Scenes,
To turn the levelled Lawns to liquid Plains,
To raise the creeping Rills from humble Beds,
And force the latent Springs to lift their Heads,
On watery Columns Capitals to rear,
That mix their flowing Curls with upper Air?
Or dost Thou, weary grown, these Works neglect,
No Temples, Statues, Obelisks erect,   30
But seek the morning Breeze from fragrant Meads,
Or shun the Noontide Ray in wholesome Shades,
Or slowly walk alone the mazy Wood,
To meditate on all that's wise and good?
For Nature, bountiful, in Thee has joined
A Person pleasing with a worthy Mind,
Not given the Form alone, but Means and Art
To draw the Eye or to allure the Heart.
Poor were the Praise in Fortune to excel,
Yet want the Way to use that Fortune well.   40
While thus adorned, while thus with Virtue crowned,
At Home in Peace, Abroad in Arms renowned,
Graceful in Form and winning in Address,
While well you think what aptly you express,
With Health, with Honour, with a fair Estate,
A Table free, and elegantly neat,
What can be added more to mortal Bliss?
What can he want who stands possessed of This?
What can the fondest wishing Mother more
Of Heaven attentive for her Son implore?   50
And yet a Happiness remains unknown,
Or to Philosophy revealed alone;
A Precept, which unpractised renders vain
Thy flowing Hopes, and Pleasure turns to Pain.
Should Hope and Fear thy Heart alternate tear,
Or Love, or Hate, or Rage, or anxious Care,
Whatever Passions may thy Mind infest,
(Where is that Mind which passions ne'er molest?)
Amid the Pangs of such intestine Strife,
Still think the Present Day thy Last of Life;   60

Defer not till to-Morrow to be wise,
To-Morrow's Sun to Thee may never rise.
Or should to-Morrow chance to cheer thy Sight
With her enlivening and unlooked-for Light,
How grateful will appear her dawning Rays,
As Favours unexpected doubly please!
Who thus can think and who such Thoughts pursues,
Content may keep his Life, or calmly lose;
A Proof of this Thou mayest thyself receive,
When Leisure from Affairs will give thee Leave.   70
Come, see thy Friend, retired without Regret,
Forgetting Cares, or trying to forget;
In easy Contemplation soothing Time
With Morals much, and now and then with Rhyme;
Not so robust in Body as in Mind,
And always undejected, though declined;
Not wondering at the World's new wicked Ways,
Compared with those of our Forefathers' Days;
For Virtue now is neither more or less,
And Vice is only varied in the Dress.   80
Believe it, Men have ever been the same,
And all the Golden Age is but a Dream.

(BL Add. MS 57804, f. 31)

In this version of the poem the spelling and punctuation, which are variable in Grenville's manuscript, follow the 1930 edition of Congreve by F.W. Bateson. The capital letters follow Curll's edition of 1729. The substantial differences of wording in Bateson's text are as follows:—

l. 4   Or *stratagems* of war, or *schemes* of state
l. 9   Does *thy* remembrance
l. 12   all *thy* victory
l. 17   *that* shame
l. 20   with *her* pen
l. 31   but *catch*
l. 33   walk *along*
l. 59   *Amidst*
l. 60   *the* last of life
l. 69   *All proofs*
l. 72   Forgetting *care*, or *striving*
l. 82   And *Ovid's* golden age

Charles, 8th Lord Cathcart (1686 – 1740)

Many of Cobham's army colleagues must have visited him in the 1720s and 1730s, but Lord Cathcart is the only one whose description of Stowe has come to light. Several things give it special interest. Nowhere else is there an account of the parkland outside the ha-ha, that extensive forest garden to the north which takes up the greater part of the 1739 plan. Nor is any other person recorded as criticising Cobham's improvements adversely to his face, a privilege perhaps reserved for an old comrade-in-arms. It may even have been the intelligence of his visitor's comments which made Cobham show him his plans for completing the gardens and then take him into the park south of the Lake Pavilions to give him an idea of how it would look. But however it happened, Cathcart's account appears to provide the first evidence of the project which, within a few years, was to turn the little valley on the eastern side into the Elysian Fields.

Charles, 8th Lord Cathcart, gained his military reputation under Marlborough in Flanders and in the 1715 campaign, especially at Sheriffmuir. He held high office under George II and in 1740 was appointed commander-in-chief of all British forces in America. He died at sea on the way to taking up his appointment.

from his *Diary*

18 August 1730. Tems comme hier.
Je revai la mist aux jardins je one levai de bonne heure ce matin pour faire le tour snet je fus des plus en plus charmé. Nelson's seat, le theatre, le batissment de Gibbs sent les pieces qui me pleurent le plus avec le vieux bois et la temple. Je trouvai le Pyramide de 60 pied bien placé mais mal executé, l'obeliske est de 70 pieds dans une piece d'eau des 2 arpents, qui va tomber par une casscade dans une grande bassin des 9 arpents. Je trouvais aussi la Rottunda, et les 2 Pavillions fort jolie. Apres dejuné Je fus faire la tour des Rydings avec my Ld dans le grass Park qui sont magnifiques. Il y a en un qu'ent [trois] miles de long et fus joints aux jeardins. Je remarquai a my Ld le peu de soin qu'il avoit a rendre la face de Park plus amies et jolie. Il anarvat que le reprimande estrit juste mais qu'il laisservit cela a ses successeurs. Je remarquai plusieures choses utiles a suivre dans les Rydings. Il me montrat ses bois qui sont vastes avec des grandes arbres avec bien de plaisir. En retournant il me montrat un peu des ses desseins pour terminer ses jardins. Son chapelain disnant chez nous. Il me montrat toute sa maison qu'est tres commaude et bien meublé et des toits de la maison les veus sont tres belles et longures. Je me promenai encore dans les jardins au soir. Je [jouai] a quadrille avec la famille. Sr Charles Tyrrill fut de la partie.

mercredi 19 tems comme hier
Je fus le matin avec Mr Grenville voir l'obelisk par un bateau. Nous fismes le trajet de bassin et montrasmes sur le Pied d'estall. Apres dejuné nous montrasmes a cheval. My Ld me montrat le Park de coté de sud avec ses dessiens pour finir ses jardins. Ce que reste a faire serat a mon avis le plus noble de toute. Il me montrat aussi son dessien pour une maison pour Coll. Speed tres charmante situation. Enfin je fus ravis de tout Lady Pemfrette avec la famille de Coll. Whiteworth disnerant chez nous. Apres disné my Ld me permit de m'en aller comblé des ses [housetetez?].

(Private collection of Earl Cathcart)

Alexander Pope (1688 – 1744)

Congreve's was not the only verse epistle addressed to Cobham. Another was composed a few years later, in 1735, by Alexander Pope, the half-title of his poem being *Of the Knowledge and Characters of Men*. It was one of a set of four "Moral Essays" which Pope wrote in the early 1730s. Cobham's gardening activities were referred to in a second poem of the set, the *Epistle to Burlington*, which dealt with the proper use of riches in building and gardening. The architectural work of Burlington was presented as a model of how to design fine buildings, and the garden of Stowe as the criterion for fine gardening.

The poem is well known, and there is no need to reprint it in full. The lines quoted here are from the passage whose climax cites Stowe as the best contemporary example of good taste in gardening. Not only are the lines among Pope's finest and memorable in themselves, but in them the major poet of his generation, himself a gardener, gave his accolade to Cobham's gardens, and there is little doubt that this was a main factor in establishing Stowe's international reputation.

Since at least 1724 Pope had included Stowe in the summer rambles he made round the houses of his aristocratic friends, and he was there in August 1731, a few months before the *Epistle to Burlington* was published. In a letter of August 23rd to John Knight he wrote: "If any thing under Paradise could set me beyond all Earthly Cogitations, Stowe might do it. It is much more beautiful this year than when I saw it before, and much enlarged, and with variety."

However, it is important to remember that the garden he so much admired was not Kent's "appearance of beautiful nature" in the Elysian Fields, but the earlier, more formal lay-out of Bridgeman, as recorded in the views which Jacques Rigaud drew in 1733. The last line of the present excerpt originally started "Lo! Bridgeman comes..." and so it remained in the first three editions, all dated 1731. But by 1735, when the next edition was published, Kent's star was rising to the zenith and Bridgeman's had waned. So Bridgeman's name was quietly replaced by Cobham's, and the poem passed safely through the gardening revolution otherwise intact.

The text follows that of the Twickenham Edition of the poems of Alexander Pope, Volume II, part 2, *Epistles to Several Persons*, edited by F.W. Bateson (1951).

from *Epistle to Burlington (1731)*

...Something there is more needful than Expence,
And something previous ev'n to Taste—'tis Sense:
Good Sense, which only is the gift of Heav'n,
And tho' no science, fairly worth the seven:
A Light, which in yourself you must perceive;
Jones and Le Nôtre have it not to give.
   To build, to plant, whatever you intend,
To rear the Column, or the Arch to bend,
To swell the Terras, or to sink the Grot;
In all, let Nature never be forgot.   50
But treat the Goddess like a modest fair,
Nor over-dress, nor leave her wholly bare;
Let not each beauty ev'ry where be spy'd,
Where half the skill is decently to hide.
He gains all points, who pleasingly confounds,
Surprizes, varies, and conceals the Bounds.
   Consult the Genius of the Place in all;
That tells the Waters or to rise, or fall,
Or helps th' ambitious Hill the heav'ns to scale,
Or scoops in circling theatres the Vale,   60
Calls in the Country, catches opening glades,
Joins willing woods, and varies shades from shades,
Now breaks, or now directs, th' intending Lines;
Paints as you plant, and, as you work, designs.
   Still follow Sense, of ev'ry Art the Soul,
Parts answ'ring parts shall slide into a whole,
Spontaneous beauties all around advance,
Start ev'n from Difficulty, strike from Chance;
Nature shall join you, Time shall make it grow
A Work to wonder at—perhaps a Stow.   70
   Without it, proud Versailles! thy glory falls;
And Nero's Terraces desert their walls:
The vast Parterres a thousand hands shall make,
Lo! Cobham comes, and floats them with a Lake...

John Loveday (1711 – 1789)

John Loveday, scholar, antiquary and connoisseur, matriculated at Magdalen College, Oxford, in 1728. It was at Oxford that he met and established a firm friendship with Thomas Hearne, vigorously defending Hearne's reputation after his death in 1735. Loveday possessed private wealth, and from Oxford he went back to his family home at Caversham, where he lived a life of studious retirement. During subsequent years he made many summer tours round Britain, keeping a detailed record in his diaries, several of which have survived.

Loveday has been well served by his descendants. In 1890 the diary of his 1732 tour was brought out in a limited edition by J.E.T. Loveday, whose granddaughter, Sarah Markham, has recently published a scholarly and lively account of her ancestor, *John Loveday of Caversham 1711-1789: The Life and Tours of an Eighteenth-Century Onlooker* (Salisbury, 1984).

For students of Stowe, he is important as a well-informed observer of the house and gardens, but his particular merit is that he went to Stowe at least three times and noted alterations which had taken place since an earlier visit. Furthermore, he was the only visitor who described the pictures in any detail during the 1730s.

The first occasion was 13 June 1729, when his brief note stated only that he and his friends met Mr. Rand, Cobham's chaplain, and that the gardens covered forty acres. But the comments he made after his later visits, on 20 May 1731 and 13 June 1735, are fuller and contain much of interest.

from his *Diaries*

20 May 1731

Lord Cobham's at Stow is a Brick Seat, placed commodiously for good Prospects. There is a Vista through the House of great length; the House is elegantly furnished; here is Tapestry of a Battle Lord Cobham was engaged in; in other Rooms, an original Picture of Oliver Cromwell in Armour with his Page; two Paintings of Van Dyck and his Wife both by Van Dyck himself, a painting of Joan D'Arc. The Rooms above Stairs were beautifying, so that we lost sight of the Pictures there. The Gardens lie most on the right of the House; no one part of them answers to another, but yet you perceive no Irregularity for the View is confined to as much only as is regular within itself; several beautiful Vistas here over an open Countrey; several Buildings, but heavy and clumsy, end the Walks, one to the memory of Sir John Vanbrugh; yet there is no Walk round this Garden; not a great deal of Water here.[1]

13 June 1735

Lord Cobham's Gardens consist of 60 Acres actually improved and kept in order; 40 acres more are also taken-in, but are not yet disposed of; the Church, Church-yard and Parsonage-house are within the Gardens. There is now also an irregular head of Water in them. Gibbs and Kent have been the Architects for the buildings in the Gardens since Sir John Vanbrugh's death. The House, as well as the Gardens, have been improved since I was here; to the middle of the Garden-front they have added a double Colonnade, one over the other, consisting of 4 Pillars each, the lower row is Tuscan, the upper Ionic; this has had a very good effect, which cannot be said of the four blunt Turrets, one at each corner, which is also a late addition. The inside of the house is wondrous elegant and is furnished accordingly. Here is excellent Tapestry of the Battle in the Wood, the old Miller appearing in it; it differs something from the Tapestry at Cliefden House, the Earl of Orkney's. Here are Tables of the Giallo antico, Paintings of Rubens's wife by Rubens, of Joan d'Arc

supposed by A. Durer, of Moses burying the Egyptian by
N. Poussin; of the marriage in Cana by Bassano; of the Duke
de Sully, French Ambassador to Charles I, a Length by Van
Dyck. Four Pictures in low life, very well done by Ciperi, now
living (if I mistake not.) Oliver Cromwell and his Page was
copied by Richardson from a Painting at the Earl of Oxford's.
The Marble Bass-Relieve of Cyrus's Camp is one of the most
exquisite pieces of Sculpture that I have ever seen. Sisygambis
is a Master-piece; the Sculptor's name appears on it.[2]

1. Markham, *op. cit., p.93*
2. *ibid., pp. 204-5*

Page 16 — *Temple of Bacchus:*

Coucher's Obelisk

Bickham Aug.t to Oct 1750

Engraving by George Bickham
from *The Beauties of Stow*

Gilbert West (1703 – 1756)

This is one of the earliest topographical poems devoted to the description of an English garden, and it is also the first of the many printed works on Stowe. West wrote it in 1731, submitting it in November of that year to Pope for "correction". Pope thought well of it, and in 1732 it was published, anonymously. It is in fact a versified guide to the gardens, the prototype of the long subsequent series published, though only once again in verse, by Seeley and others. The guides all follow, more or less, West's route round the gardens.

Gilbert West, one of the most gifted of Cobham's nephews, was a good classical scholar, and it is likely that he was a main contributor to the iconography of the gardens. So it is not surprising that all the information he gives in his poem (and in its footnotes) has proved to be correct. He writes as a guest in the house, starting his circuit of the gardens from the steps of the mansion and picking up the tourist route only when he reaches the visitor's entrance by the Lake Pavilions. His poem is therefore key evidence for the history of Stowe's gardens.

A minor puzzle has been solved by the copy of the poem in Princeton University Library. After visiting the Temple of Bacchus, West breaks off to tell the story of the pretty girl on a swing who stirs the passions of an onlooker and is chased across the garden to a "private grotto", which West inexplicably calls the "Randibus" — perhaps a corruption of the regular garden feature known as a 'rondibus', or 'rond-point'. The name of the man in the affair is left blank, though West says that he is too good-natured to mind the tale's being told against him. In the Princeton copy someone has written "Rand" over the blanks, with a manuscript note below that he was the minister at Stowe; and from 1711 until his death in 1734 the vicar of Stowe was indeed Conway Rand. Little else is known about him, except that he was chaplain of Cobham's regiment and almost certainly the clergyman who looked after the greyhound Signor Fido in his old age.

At about the date of the poem Dido's Cave was built at, or near, the Randibus, which must have been intended to commemorate this disreputable incident, since West's description consciously echoes several lines from Virgil's *Aeneid IV*. Not far away stood the obelisk to Robert Coucher, another of Cobham's regimental chaplains and also mentioned in West's poem, who appears to have been a parson of the same humour.

The text follows the edition of 1732.

STOWE,
The Gardens of the Right Honourable Richard Lord Viscount Cobham (1732)

To Thee, great Master of the vocal String,
O Pope, of Stowe's Elyzian Scenes I sing:
That Stowe, which better far thy Muse divine
Commands to live in one distinguish'd Line.[1]
Yet let not thy superior Skill disdain
The friendly Gift of this Poetick Plan.
The same presiding Muse alike inspires
The Planter's Spirit and the Poet's Fires,
Alike, unless the Muse propitious smile,
Vain is the Planter's, vain the Poet's Toil.   10
All great, all perfect Works from Genius flow,
The British Iliad hence, and hence the Groves of Stowe.
   To guardian Phoebus the first Strains belong,
(And may th' auspicious Omen bless the Song)
To Phoebus, and th' attendant Virgin Train,[2]
That o'er each Verse, each learned Science reign,
And round embellishing the gay Parterre,
Unite their sacred Influences here.
Here Congreve, welcome Guest, oft chear'd the Days,
With friendly Converse, or poetick Lays.   20
Here Lyttleton oft spreads his growing Wing,
Delighted in these Shades to rove and sing.
And Thou, where Thames impels his silver Flood,
Quitting the Care of thy own rising Wood,
Oft, as thy Breast, with pleasing Rapture glow'd,
Hast here, O Pope, avow'd th' inspiring God.
In a green Niche's over-arching Shrine,
Each tuneful Goddess shrouds her Form divine.
Beneath, in the wide Area's middle Space,
A jetting Fount its chrystal Flood displays.   30

1. See Epistle to the Earl of Burlington.
2. Statues of Apollo, the Nine Muses, and the Liberal Arts and Sciences placed round the Parterre.

In whose clear Face again reflected shine
Pierian Phoebus, and the Virgin Nine.
Here too for ever bloom th' Aonian Bays,[3]
Ordain'd the Meed of tuneful Poets' Lays.
In seemly Order They on either Hand,
Alternate in the verdant Arches stand:
Alternate glitt'ring with the gilded Vase,
On either Hand the verdant Arches blaze.
Here, odorous Flowers perfume the vital Gale,
And here Hesperian Oranges exhale.[4]   40
Transported hence the Summer-hearth they grace,
And shine, collected in the China Vase;
Or on the Sunday's consecrated Morn,
Select in Nosegays the fair Breast adorn.
      Lead thro' the Circle,[5] Virgins, lead me on,
Where, guided by the still-revolving Sun,
The faithful Dial counts the fleeting Hour,
Lead to the Church's venerable Tower:
Which like the life-producing Plant of Old,
That flourish'd once in Eden's blessed Mould,   50
In the mid-Garden placed, its sacred Head
Uprears, embosom'd in aspiring Shade:
And blest with Vertue, like that wond'rous Tree,
Confers on Mortals Immortality.
      Hence thro' the Windings of the mazy Wood
Descending, lo! the Octagon's clear Flood,
And rustick Obelisk's aerial Height,
Burst in one sudden View upon the Sight.
Batavian Poplars here in ranks ascend;[6]
Like some high Temple's arching Isles extend   60
The taper Trunks, a living Colonnade;
Eternal Murmur animates the Shade.

3. Bay-Trees and gilt Vases, placed alternately in the Arches of the
   Arcade.
4. The Orangerie.
5. The Sun-Dial Parlour.
6. The Abeal Walk.

Above, two Dorick Edifices[7] grace
An elevated Platform's utmost Space;
From whence, beyond the Brook that creeps below,
Along yon beauteous Hill's green sloping Brow,
The Garden's destin'd Boundaries extend,
Where Cobham's pleasing Toils, tho' late, shall end;
Beneath the far-stretch'd Lake's capacious Bed,
Receives the loud, praecipitate Cascade;   70
And tufted Groves along the verdant Side,
Cast their deep Shadows o'er the silver Tide:
The silver Tide (where yonder high-rais'd Mound
Forms the wide-floating Lake's extremest Bound)
In secret Channels thro' the swelling Hill,
Gives Force and Motion to th' impulsive Wheel;
Whose constant Whirl, the spouting Jets supplies,
And bids aloft th' unwilling Waters rise.
Fair on the Brow, a spacious Building stands,
Th' applauded Work of Kent's judicious Hands: 80
The spreading Wings in arched Circles bend,
And rustick Domes each arched Circle end.
Thence back returning, thro' the narrow Glade,
See, where the Ruin[8] lifts its mould'ring Head!
Within, close-shelter'd from the peering Day,
Satyrs and Fauns their wanton Frolicks play.
While sad Malbecco in the secret Cell,
Hears each rude Monster "ring his Matin's Bell."[9]
    Where yon high Firs display their darksome Green,
And mournful Yews compose a solemn Scene,   90
Around thy Building, Gibbs, a sacred Band[10]

7. Two Pavilions built by Sir J. Vanbrugh.
8. The Ruin, painted on the Inside with the Story of Malbecco, out
   of Spencer's Fairy Queen, Book 3. Canto 10.
9. An Hemystick of Spencer.
10. Alluding to the Inscription on the Building.
    Hic Manus, ob Patriam pugnando Vulnera passi;
    Quique pii Vates, & Phoebo digna locuti;
    Inventas aut qui Vitam excoluere per Artes;
    Quique sui memores alios fecere merendo. Virg. Lib. 6.

Of Princes, Patriots, Bards, and Sages stand:
Men, who by Merit purchas'd lasting Praise,
Worthy each British Poet's noblest Lays:
Or bold in Arms for Liberty they stood,
And greatly perish'd for their Country's Good:
Or nobly warm'd with more than mortal Fire,
Equal'd to Rome and Greece the British Lyre:
Or Human Life by useful Arts refin'd,
Acknowledg'd Benefactors of Mankind.   100
    Thou first Elizabeth, Imperial Maid,
By freeborn Subjects willingly obey'd;
Foe to the Tyranny of Spain, and Rome,
Abroad respected, and belov'd at home.
Beneath the friendly Shelter of thy Throne
Each Art of Peace with useful Lustre shone:
Industrious Commerce courted every Gale,
And spread in distant Worlds her fearless Sail.
Encourag'd Science rear'd her laurel'd Head,
And all the pleasing Train of Muses led.   110
Lo! Verulam and Shakespear near Thee stand,
Rais'd by thy Smiles to grace this happy Land:
Both dear to Phoebus, sacred both to Fame,
With Princes here an equal Rank they claim;
This with the richest Stores of Learning fraught,
That by indulgent Nature only taught.
All hail! auspicious Queen, thy Praise shall live
(If Worth like thine Eternity can give)
When no proud Bust th' Imperial Wreath shall bear,
And Brass and Marble waste to Dust and Air.   120
    O! that like Thee, succeeding Kings had strove,
To build their Empire on their People's Love!
That taught by thy Example they had known,
That only Justice can support a Throne!
Then had not Britain wanted Hambden's Hand,
Weak and oppressive Counsels to withstand:
Nor had the Patriot, on his native Plain,
Dy'd for the Laws he struggled to maintain.
Behold his Bust with Civick Honours grac'd,

Detail of engraving by Jacques Rigaud
View from Gibbs's Building

Nearest to thine, immortal Nassau plac'd,   130
To thine, great William, whose protecting Sword,
That Liberty, for which He fell, restor'd.
   Next Locke, who in defence of Conscience rose,
And strove religious Rancour to compose:
Justly opposing every human Test,
Since God alone can judge who serves him best.
   But what is he, in whom the heav'nly Mind
Shines forth distinguish'd and above Mankind?
This, this is Newton; He, who first survey'd
The Plan, by which the Universe was made: 140
Saw Nature's simple, yet stupendous Laws,
And prov'd th' Effects, tho' not explain'd the Cause.
   Thou too, bold Milton, whose immortal Name,
Thy Country dares to match with Homer's Fame;
Whose tow'ring Genius vast and unconfin'd,
Left ev'n the Limits of the World behind;
Thro' Hell, thro' Chaos, and infernal Night,
Ascending to the Realms of purest Light;
Or else on Earth, in Eden's happy Grove,
With Peace, with Bliss conversing, and with Love: 150
Here art thou plac'd, these blooming shades among,
Second to those alone thy Muse has sung.
   An ancient Wood[11] (upon whose topmost Bough
High-waving croaks the unauspicious Crow)
From hence its venerable Gloom extends,
Where, rivalling its lofty Height, ascends
The pointed Pyramid: This too is thine,
Lamented Vanbrugh! This thy last Design.
Among the various Structures, that around,
Form'd by thy Hand, adorn this happy Ground,   160
This, sacred to thy Memory shall stand:[12]
Cobham, and grateful Friendship so command.

11. The Rook-Spinny.
12. Alluding to the Inscription, *Inter Plurima Hortorum horunce Aedificia a Johanne Vanbrugh Equite designata Hanc Pyramidem illius Memoriae sacram esse voluit Cobham.*

Nysean Bacchus next the Muse demands;
To Him, in yon high Grove, a Temple stands;[13]
Where British Oaks their ancient Arms display,
Impervious to the Sun's unclouded Ray,
There, half-conceal'd, it rears its Rustick Head;
The painted Walls mysterious Orgies spread.[14]
A jolly Figure on the Cieling reels,
Whose every Nerve the potent Goblet feels: 170
His Vine-bound Brows bespeak him God of Wine,
The Cheeks, and swelling Paunch, O! ——* are thine.
—— (not unknown to Phoebus is the Name)
Once felt the Fervour of a softer Flame;
When heedless Fortune shot the sudden Dart,
And unexpected Rapture seiz'd his Heart.
My faithful Verse this Secret shall reveal,
Nor —— himself shall blame the mirthful Tale.
    A cool Recess there is, not far away,
Sacred to Love, to Mirth, and rural Play.   180
Hither oftimes the youthful Fair resort,
To cheat the tedious Hours with various Sport.
Some mid the Nine-pins marshall'd Orders roll,
With Aim unerring the impetuous Bowl.
Others, whose Souls to loftier Objects move,
Delight the Swing's advent'rous Joys to prove:
While on each side the ready Lovers stand,
The flying Cord obeys th' impulsive Hand.
As on a Day contending Rivals strove,
By manly Strength to recommend their Love;   190
Toss'd to and fro, up flew the giddy Fair,
And scream'd, and laugh'd, and play'd in upper Air.
The flutt'ring Coats the rapid Motion find,
And One by One admit the swelling Wind:
At length the last, white, subtle Veil withdrew,
And those mysterious Charms expos'd to view—

13. The rustick Temple, built by Sir J. Vanbrugh.
14. Rites and Revels of Bacchus.
*   *[The omitted name is that of Conway Rand, the Vicar of Stowe.]*

44

Engraving by George Bickham from *The Beauties of Stow*

What Transport then, O —— possess'd thy Soul!
Down from thy Hand, down dropt the idle Bowl:
As for the skilful Tip prepar'd he stood,
And Hopes and Fears alarm'd th' expecting Croud.   200
Sudden to seize the beauteous Prey he sprung;
Sudden with Shrieks the echoing Thicket rung.
Confounded and abash'd, the frighted Maid,
(While rising Blushes ting'd her Cheeks with red)
Fled swift away, more rapid than the Wind,
And left the treach'rous Swing, and —— behind,
Down the smooth Lawn she flew with eager Haste,
And near thy Obelisk,[15] O Coucher, pass'd:
As on the wounded Stone thy Name she view'd,
The well-known Name her every Fear renew'd;   210
And strait, in dreadful Vision, to her Eyes
She sees another Priest and Lover rise.
Nor cou'd thy gentle Mind her Fears assuage,
Nor honest Heart, that knew nor Guile nor Rage;
But with redoubled speed away she fled,
And sought the Shelter of the closer Shade;
Where in thick Covert, to her weary Feet,
A Private Grotto[16] promis'd safe Retreat:
Alas! too private, for too safely there
The fierce Pursuer seiz'd the helpless Fair;   220
The Fair he seiz'd, while round him all the Throng
Of laughing Dryads, Hymenaeals sung:
Pronubial Juno gave the mystick Sign,
And Venus nodded from her neighb'ring Shrine.[17]
The Grotto, conscious of the happy Flame,
From this auspicious Deed derives its Name.
    Here future Lovers, when in Troops they come,
Venus, to visit thy distinguish'd Dome,
As thro' this consecrated Shade they pass,
Shall offer to the Genius of the Place.   230

15. An Obelisk, in Memory of Robin Coucher.
16. The Randibus.
17. The Rotunda.

Shift now the closer Scene: and view around,
With various Beauties the wide Landskip crown'd.
Here level Glades extend their length'ning Lines,
There in just Order the deep Quincunce shines.
Here chrystal Lakes reflect contiguous Shades,
There distant Hills uplift their azure Heads.
Round the free Lawn[18] here gadding Heifers stray,
And frisking Lambs in sportive Gambols play.
There murmur to the Wind Groves ever-green,
And inter-mingled Buildings rise between: 240
The Sun declin'd with milder Glory burns,
And the fair Piece with various Light adorns.
Lo! in the Centre of this beauteous Scene,
Glitters beneath her Dome[19] the Cyprian Queen:
Not like to her, whom ancient Homer prais'd,
To whom a thousand sacred Altars blaz'd:
When simple Beauty was the only Charm,
With which each tender Nymph and Swain grew warm:
But, yielding to the now-prevailing Taste,
In Gold, for modern Adoration, drest.   250
For her the Naiads, in their watry Bed,
Amid the level Green a Mirror spread;[20]
Along whose terrass'd Banks the shelt'ring Wood,
Defends from ruder Winds th' unruffled Flood.
       Beyond, a sylvan Theatre[21] displays
Its circling Bosom to the Noon-tide Rays.
In Shade, o'er Shade, the sloping Ranks ascend,
And tall Abeals the steep Gradation end.
Here to the Sun the glossy Laurels shine,
There wave the darker Honours of the Pine.   260
       High on a Pedestal, whose swelling Base,
To Heav'n itself aspiring Columns raise,

18. A large Field encompass'd with the Garden.
19. The Rotunda, on Pillars of the Ionic Order, with an Altar of blue
    Marble, and gilded Statue of the Venus of Medicis.
20. The Rotunda Pond.
21. The Queen's Theatre, with Her Majesty's Statue erected on four Columns.

Shines the great Part'ner of Augustus' Bed,
The guardian Goddess of the noble Shade.
Beneath, in order ranged on either hand,
Attendant Nymphs and Swains rejoycing stand.
    But cou'd the Muse presume her lowly Pray'r
Might win attention from the Royal Ear,
Here shou'd those Princely Stars, that dawning smile,
With kindly Lustre on Britannia's Isle,   270
Fair Constellation! in one Blaze unite,
Aiding with filial Beams their Mother's Light.
Here shou'd Imperial Caroline be seen,
The glorious Rival of the Phrygian Queen,[22]
Who 'mid the thousand Altars that around,
Blaz'd in old Rome's Pantheon, high enthron'd,
With Pride survey'd the venerable Dome,
Fill'd with the heav'nly Off-spring of her Womb.
    And see! where, elevated far above,
A Column[23] overlooks yon nodding Grove;   280
On which, the Scene of Glory to compleat,
Deck'd with the Ensigns of Imperial State,
Stands the great Father, George, whose equal Sway,
With Joy Britannia's happy Realms obey.
Thence round, he views the cultivated Plain,
That smiling speaks the Blessings of his Reign.
Thus, o'er their Planets radiant Suns preside,
By Heav'n's fixt Laws their various Courses guide;
And shedding round Benevolence divine,
Bless'd by depending Worlds, indulgent shine.   290
    Deep in this close, umbrageous, wild Recess,
Where the sweet Songsters of the feather'd Race,
Warble their native Musick thro' the Shade;
A solitary Building[24] hides its Head.
This peaceful Fabrick, for Repose design'd,
Close Valves defend from penetrating Wind;

22. Cybele, Mother of the Gods.
23. The King's Pillar and Statue.
24. The Sleeping-House.

And the thick Under-wood's combining Boughs,
On every Side a verd'rous Wall compose.
Nigh, sound the quiv'ring Poplars in the Air,
Like falling Waters murm'ring from afar.   300
Here, where their quiet unmolested Reign
The Gods of Sleep and Solitude maintain;
Whether soft Slumbers close thy languid Eyes,
Or Thought be lost in pleasing Réveries,
From yon sage Motto[25] learn thy self to spare,
And bid adieu to unavailing Care.
Let not the Censures of the Wise dismay;
But where thy own clear Reason leads the Way,
Her pleasing Dictates uncontroll'd pursue,
Thy Dreams, may be as good as Theirs, perhaps as true. 310
     Forsaking now the Covert of the Maze,
Along the broader Walk's more open Space,
Pass we to where a sylvan Temple spreads
Around the Saxon Gods, its hallow'd Shades.
     Hail! Gods of our renown'd Fore-Fathers, hail!
Ador'd Protectors once of England's Weal.
Gods, of a Nation, valiant, wise, and free,
Who conquer'd to establish Liberty!
To whose auspicious Care Britannia owes
Those Laws, on which she stands, by which she rose. 320
Still may your Sons that noble Plan pursue,
Of equal Government prescrib'd by you.
Nor e'er indignant may you blush to see,
The Shame of your corrupted Progeny!
     First radiant Sunna shews his beamy Head,
Mona to Him, and scepter'd Tiw succeed;
Tiw, ancient Monarch of remotest Fame,
Who led from Babel's Tow'rs the German Name.
And warlike Woden, fam'd for martial Deeds,
From whom great Brunswick's noble Line proceeds. 330
Dread Thuner see! on his Imperial Seat,
With awful Majesty, and kingly State

25. *Cum Omnia sint in incerto fave Tibi.*

Reclin'd! at his Command black Thunders roll,
And Storms and fiery Tempests shake the Pole.
With various Emblem next fair Friga charms,
Array'd in female Stole and manly Arms,
Expressive Image of that Double Soul,
Prolifick Spirit that informs the Whole;
Whose Genial Power throughout exerts its Sway,
And Earth, and Sea, and Air, its Laws obey.   340
Last of the Circle hoary Seatern stands;
Instructive Emblems fill his mystick Hands.
In this a Wheel's revolving Orb declares
The never-ending Round of rolling Years,
That holds a Vessel fill'd with fading Flowers
And Fruits collected by the ripening Hours.
Be warn'd from hence, ye Fair Ones! to improve
The transitory Minutes made for Love,
E're yet th' inexorable Hand of Time
Robs of its bloomy Sweets your lovely Prime.   350
    Lo, Nelson's airy Seat, whose rising Sides
Obscuring Fir, and shining Laurel hides!
Here in sweet Contrast Rural Scenes display'd
Around their native wilder Beauties spread.
The tufted Woodlands, where the Hunter's Horn
Oft wakes with chearful Note the drowzy Morn;
The Brook that glitters in the Vale below,
And all the rising Lawn's enlightened Brow,
In lowly Huts[26] adown whose shelving Side,
From Storms secure the peaceful Hinds reside: 360
The spacious Park, within whose circling Pale,
The bounding Deer at large imprison'd dwell;
And feed in social Herds along the Glade,
Or lonely seek the solitary Shade.
Far o'er the level Green, in just array,
Long Rows of Trees their adverse Fronts display.
So when two Nations, fierce in Arms, prepare
At one decisive Stroke to end the War,

26. The Village of Dadford.

In seemly Order, e'er the Battle joins,
The marshal'd Hosts extend their threat'ning Lines,   370
And Files to Files oppos'd await the Word,
That gives a Loose to the destroying Sword.
   High on a Mount, amid a verdant Field,
Where intermitted Lines wide opening yield;
Where from their plenteous Urns the watry Gods
Pour o'er the green expanse their limpid Floods,
Behold the good old King in Armour clad,[27]
Triumphant Wreaths his sacred Temples shade.
And in his gracious Aspect shine exprest,
The manly Beauties of his gentle Breast;   380
His Mind, sincere, benevolent and great,
Nor aw'd by Danger, nor with Pow'r elate;
For Valour much, but more for Justice known,
Brave in the Field, and Good upon the Throne.
   An ample Arch,[28] beneath whose spacious Round,
The massy Valves on turning Hinges sound,
Opens its hospitable Bosom wide;
Thro' which at large the rolling Chariots glide.
On swelling Bastions here Two Buildings rise,[29]
(While far beneath the low-sunk Valley lies;   390
Where, or in one broad Lake the Waters spread,
Or draw their humid Trains along the Mead.)
Of These, a Shelter from the scorching Rays,
One in the Garden spreads his rustick Base:
One in the Park, an habitable Frame,
The Household Lares, and Penates claim.

27. Equestrian Statue of George I at the Head of the Canal, with this Inscription,

   In medio mihi Caesar erit,
   Et viridi in Campo Signum de Marmore ponam
   Propter Aquam.   Virg.

28. The great Entrance into the Park, and approach to the House along the Garden Wall.

29. Two Buildings, call'd Boycut Buildings, on each side the Entrance. One in the Garden, the other in the Park was intended for a House for Colonel Speed, deceas'd.

But shall the Muse approach the Pile, assign'd
Once, for a Mansion to her much-lov'd Friend,
And not bestow one sad, one tuneful Tear,
Unhappy Speed! on thy untimely Bier?   400
Here, had not hasty Fate our Hopes deceiv'd,
In sweet Retirement tranquil had'st thou liv'd;
And pass'd with him, whose Friendship did ingage
In Arms thy Youth, in Peace thy weary Age.
Faithful Companion of his toilsome Days,
He led Thee on in Glory's noble Chace!
Faithful Companion of his calm Retreat,
Here had he destin'd thy delightful Seat.
Here too the Muse had joy'd to see thee blest,
Of every Hope, of every Wish possest;   410
Had sung, with Friendship and Affection mov'd,
Thy honest Heart by all esteem'd and lov'd;
And to thy living Worth that Tribute paid,
Which sorrowing now she offers to thy Shade.

George Vertue (1684 – 1756)

For many years George Vertue, the engraver and antiquary, collected information for a projected history of the arts in England. The book was never written, but Vertue's notes were used by Horace Walpole in his *Anecdotes of Painting*, and the notebooks themselves, now in the British Library, have been published in six volumes between 1930 and 1947 by the Walpole Society (Vols. 18, 20, 22, 24, 26 and 29). It is from these that the passages on Stowe have been drawn.

Two of the extracts, numbers two and four, record actual visits to the house and gardens. Vertue added very little in the way of comment, which is all the more regrettable as both occasions were associated with visits to the famous Buckinghamshire antiquary, Browne Willis, and we would very much like to know what these two had to say to each other on the subject of Stowe.

But though Vertue was reticent about the place itself, he was much more forthcoming on the set of engravings which Jacques Rigaud was commissioned to make of Cobham's gardens in 1733. Extracts three and five tell us most of what we know about Bridgeman's magnificent but financially disastrous scheme.

As the first extract indicates, Vertue saw a copy of Gilbert West's *Stowe* almost as soon as it was published. Elsewhere in his notebooks (III, p.70) he copied out three passages from the poem, twenty-one lines in all, commenting only that the busts of the eight original British Worthies were "made by Mr Rysbrake". He was also an early purchaser of Seeley's guidebook, buying a copy of the second edition (1745), which he correctly described as "a small book printed and sold in Buckingham". From this he extracted a mass of detailed information for his notebook, but only two sentences were not based directly on the guidebook, and these alone have been reprinted as extract six. He must have known Seeley personally, since a few years later he engraved five plates for the illustrated views of Stowe which Seeley published in 1750.

Too much reliance should not be placed on the dating of the extracts. The casual arrangement of Vertue's notebooks and his habit of correcting earlier entries when new information came to hand make some of the dates uncertain.

from his *Notebooks*

1.   [1732] Lord Cobhams—a Poem calld Stowe by Mr West, a nephew of Lord Cobhams. In the Gardens. Temple of the Gods. Temple of the Worthies. A Pyramid—a Rotunda. Venus in the Middle. Temple of Morpheus—the Hermitage. Collumna Regia. 4 Columna Reginas. 2 pavillions. 1 pavillion Gibbs. Great Collum and bason.

(V, p.103)

2.   1732 Sunday July 16—with my Friend Mr Grimbalston set out, dynd at St Albans, lay at Dunstable—next day dind with Brown Willis Esq. at his house [at] Bleachly. See the Church—Lay at Whaddon Mr Willis house—next day See a decayd large house called Salden... Next to Buckingham and so on to Lord Cobhams whose gardens are delightfull and magnificent, his house noble, richly furnisht. From thence to Towcester.

(V, p.103)

3.   1733. Monsieur Rigaud about February from Paris came over here at the request of Mr. Bridgman, the Kings Gardner, to be employd by him to make designs of Gardens, Views, etc of which at Lord Cobhams he has been some time, made many drawings most excellently performd. He being perfect Master of perspective finely disposes his groups of Trees, light and shade and figures in a masterly manner—some of the plates he has begun to Engrave which is his Excellency also.

(III, p.69)

4.   1734 I made a Tour with Roger Gale Esqr. to St Albans, Dunstable, Northampton, Warwick, Whaddon, B.Willis etc. Lord Cobhams house and Gardens. There are the designs of Sir J. Vanbrugg, Mr Kent and Mr Gibbs in the

Gardens, the Temples, rotundas, the Hermitage, Pavillions, Columna Georgiana and Caroline.

$\frac{1}{2}$ len[gth] of ..., Knight of the Bath, Dyke.
Amphitrion and Socia, Rembrand.
Oliver Cromwell and page, ...
Stanyan, a half len[gth], hat and Feather, a spear in his hand, said to be done by Car. Johnson.
The Hall in Chiaro Scuro by Kent.

(IV, p.37)

5.   1736. Four large Views or prospects of Palaces– Greenwich, St James Park, Hampton Court, Richmond—drawn and Engravd by Rigaud (a print also a prospect the Inside of St James Chapel marriage of the Princess of Wales) who came over into England, was imployd to draw views for the Earl of Burlington, Duke of Newcastle and for Lord Cobham Gardens in many views. Staid here about 12 or 18 months and returnd to Paris, leaving Mr Bridgmans works not intirely finishd. But Baron, who did part of it, managed it so as to get him away and got the finishing part to himself, but Bridgeman dyd before it was published—

This work consisting of 16 plates, all the draughts drawn by... Rigaud highly finished. And although Baron has in the writing joynd his name to both drawing and Engraving, Baron only gravd—

No.3 of the large prints

View from the portico of the house	No.5	
View of the Gibbs building	7	of the
View of the lesser obelisk	13	small
View from Nelsons Seat	9	

The General plan by another graver—the whole sett sold and subscribd for four guineas, published 1739.

(VI, p.194)

6.   Description of Lord Cobhams Gardens at Stowe 1745.

An Egyptian Pyramid 60 feet high to the memory of Sir John Vanbrugh, who was most concernd in the direction of Lord Cobhams (Gardens) or rather buildings because Mr Bridgeman, Gardiner to the King, had the direction and disposition of the Gardens.

A Saxon Temple, round it seven deities who gave name to the days of the week cut in stone, done by Mr Rysbrackt.

(III, p.133)

Browne Willis (1682 – 1760)

Browne Willis, of Whaddon Hall near Bletchley, in his later years a noted eccentric in dress and manner, was an indefatigable antiquary, local historian and conservationist. He is said to have visited every cathedral in England and Wales except Carlisle, and was a pioneer in basing his work on records and registers. Having served as M.P. for Buckingham 1705-8, he came to have a peculiar affection for the town and tried hard to get the spire of its church restored. This landmark, on which Cobham's father, Sir Richard Temple, had aligned his new house at Stowe in 1678, collapsed twenty years later and was never rebuilt, in spite of Browne Willis's efforts.

Whatever he may have thought of Stowe's owners in private, he was always respectful in print, no doubt realising that any improvements he contemplated for Buckingham would require their support. These feelings appear to be just under the surface of the introductory paragraph on Stowe in his *History and Antiquities of the Town, Hundred, and Deanery of Buckingham*, which was finally published in 1755.

Browne Willis's printer, unable to find type which would express the Anglo-Saxon word for 'Stow', fell back on a Greek fount, which is reproduced here.

Added below are two manuscript notes written in the margin of his own copy of the *History*. The first of these entries records preparatory arrangements for laying out the Elysian Fields.

from *History and Antiquities of the Town, Hundred, and Deanery of Buckingham (1755)*

STOW,

So called from the *Saxon* Word δτορ, which signifies a Place, as *Godstowe, Brightstow,* &c. as indeed this may, by way of Eminence, be properly so entitled; for the Situation of it is not to be exceeded; it having all the Ornaments of Nature, to which have been added those of Art, to render the Mansion Seat and Gardens of its Lord one of the Wonders of the Kingdom: As has been elegantly set forth in two incomparable Poems; one on the Description of the said Gardens by *Gilbert West,* Esq; late Student of *Christ Church, Oxford,* printed *Anno* 1732; and the other on the Subject of *Taste,* by the celebrated Mr. *Pope*; who hath inscribed it to the Right Honurable the Lord *Cobham,* who has thus exquisitely adorned it, insomuch as nothing seems wanting to render its Beauty compleat, in all Respects, except the re-edifying the tall Spire Steeple of *Bucks,* heretofore one of its principal Views; which would redound to the singular Honour of this County, and remain a standing Monument of Affection to the Mother Town, and beyond all other Illustrations dignify the antient Family Motto,

TEMPLA QUAM DILECTA.

(p. 273)

[Anno] 1732 or 1733 the vicarage House was exchanged. It is now situated in the South East Corner of the Garden Wall. The House contains 3 Roods, there is a close of 4 acres and 2 cows commons allotted in Lieu of Privy Tythes for the Hamlet of Boycot when it was annexed to Stow parish.

(p. 280, in margin)

In the year 1742 the walls of the church were white washed and the Ld's Prayer creed and commandments painted on the Walls and the King's Arms drawn and framd and hung up in Mr Gabell['s vestry room].

(p. 281, in margin)

Anonymous
probably John Whaley (1710 – 1745)

According to William Cole, the Cambridge antiquary, who was lent the journal and transcribed it in 1775, John Dodd of King's College, afterwards M.P. for Reading, made his tour in the late summer of 1735 with Francis Shepheard, another Cambridge undergraduate. Two older men went with them, Mr. Riske and Mr. Whaley, then a Fellow of King's, who wrote the journal of their tour. John Whaley, who was born and died in Norwich, also wrote a topographical poem, "A Journey to Houghton", which was printed in *A Collection of Original Poems and Translations* (London, 1745).

Among his prefatory remarks Cole wrote: "Altho' a great Part of the Journal seems to be mere common-Place and trite Observations, I shall nevertheless transcribe the Whole, as I find it: and only add, that of all the Men I was ever acquainted with, the Writer of this Journal was the most abandoned and worthless, and the most unfit to be trusted with the Education of a young Gentleman, whose Morals he was sure to corrupt."

It was on 19 September 1735 that this intriguing party of tourists arrived at Stowe, but, as Cole has warned us, the record of their visit is disappointingly commonplace.

from *Journal of John Dodd's Tour (1735)*

Within 2 Miles of Buckingham is Stowe, the Seat and Gardens of the Lord Cobham; which last are esteemed the finest of their kind in England; and are indeed most elegantly disposed, and beautifully diversifyed with Walks and Lawns, Canals and Grotto's, Waterfalls and various Buildings, such as Temples, Rotundas, Pyramids, Obelisks and Colonnades: in short you find here beautifull Nature improved by happy Art.

(BL Add. MS 5842, f. 130)

Jeremiah Milles (1714 – 1784)

More interesting and far more useful than Dodd's journal is the account of Jeremiah Milles, who examined the gardens a few weeks earlier, on 25 July 1735. Milles had been educated at Eton and Corpus Christi, Oxford, taking his B.A. in 1733 and his M.A. in 1735. During the 1730s he made several visits to the continent with the indefatigable traveller Richard (later Bishop) Pococke, his cousin, and throughout his life he kept journals of the tours he made round the British Isles. Elected F.S.A. in 1741 and F.R.S. in 1742, he became Dean of Exeter in 1762 and President of the Society of Antiquaries in 1768.

Seldom has Stowe had so learned and observant a visitor. Elsewhere in the journal of his 1735 tour he quoted the opinions of Camden and Stukely, copied out word for word a number of epitaphs and other inscriptions (including several in Greek), and lamented that the person who showed him round Althorp was so ignorant about the famous pictures. At Stowe he was the first to describe the Elysian Fields in any detail, at a time when only nine of the sixteen British Worthies were yet in position, and when building the Temple of Ancient Virtue had not even started. He left half a page free to insert the spoof epitaph to Signor Fido, though he never managed to get hold of the text, and so the page remains blank; and when he came to write up his account of Nelson's Seat, it seems that he could not read his own notes, for he confused two of the inscriptions. If ever there was an argument for a printed guidebook to record such details, this was it. But, as yet, none was available.

from *An Account, of the Journey that Mr Hardness and I took in July 1735*

We sett out from Oxford on Friday the 25th of July... From hence [Tingewick] we went 2 miles more to Stow the seat of the Lord Cobham in all 20 miles. This house and gardens is situated in the middle of an agreable Park. The gardens here are accounted the finest in England, they now contain an 100 acres My Lord having enclos'd 40 acres very lately. The house is built of Brick, and has a double front. That towards the gardens has a double-story'd Portico in the middle, the lower supported by 4 Dorick, and the upper by four Ionick Corinthian Pillars. The other front has a single story'd Portico, which is of the same heigh with the other two it is supported by 4 Ionick Pillars. Before the front of the house opens a Parterre which is clos'd on each side by trees, cut in Arcades, under which stand gilt vases, and Bay trees alternately. Towards the bottom are the statues of Apollo, and the nine Muses. From hence a green slope with a row Poplars on each side leads down to an Octogon piece of water, in the middle of which stands a rusticated obelisk of stone upon an arch. Just beyond this rises a slope, which is the extremity of the garden, where stand 2 similar open Temples of the dorick order built by Sir John Vanbrugh, supported by 4 pillars in front, and 2 on each side. The walls are painted al Fresco with two storys out of Pastor fido. A little distance from hence is a cold bath lin'd on the inside with dutch tiles of about 4 feet in depth.

Farther on with its front towards a lake, which is supply'd with water from the Octogon, stands a little hermitage, (formerly design'd for the ruins). The outside is rough, over the door is carved a Syrinx and by it a little tower as if design'd for a bell; the inside is plain having 3 niches in which are as many seats.

The next building situated at the corner of the lake is what they call the Persian Pavillion built by Kent. Its figure is semicircular. This consists of a middle building and a [small] square pavillion at each side joind by a Portico. That in the middle is semicircular without, cross which goes an entablature, which is supported by 2 pillars of the Ionick order; there are 6 or 8 niches in which are busts. Within is a square Room. On one side of it is this inscription

Veneri Hortensi.

It has a Cove ceiling which was then about to be painted by Slaughter.

At another corner of the lake on a mount stands a square building with a Butrice at each corner, and 2 sides of it open, it was formerly the Temple of the Worthys and the verses are carv'd on the back of it

Hic manus ob patriam pugnando vulnera passi Etc.

It is now call'd the Belvedere.

Above this at the upper end of a walk stands a Pyramid of 60 feet high built by and dedicated to the memory of Sir John Vanbrugh. Round it is this inscription

Inter plurima hortorum horuncce aedificia a Joh: Vanbrugh Equite designata hanc Pyramidem illius memoriae sacram esse voluit Cobham

Within are these verses

Lusisti satis, edisti satis, atque bibisti;
Tempus abire tibi est, ne potum largius aequo
Rideat et pulset lasciva decentius aetas.

At the other end of the Pyramid walk is a statue of Hercules and Antaeus, in lead by Carpenter good.

At the grand entrance into the garden stand two square Pavillions built by Gibbs, one call'd Boycots building. The other answering to it was design'd for a house for Colonel Speed. Boycots building within is a square room. In 4 niches att the corners stands the statues in lead, of Cicero, M. Aurelius, Livia and Faustina. Between these 2 buildings are a very handsome pair of iron gates made by Kent.

We came next into a triangular grass-plot, at the bottom of which is an obelisk dedicated to one Coucher a clergyman, and therefore call'd Couchers Obelisk, and at the top is a rustick temple of brick dedicated to Bacchus. It has 3 doors in front, and one on each side. It is painted on the inside al Fresco with the Orgys of Bacchus.

Next to this we came to what they call the Sylvan temple dedicated to the Saxon Gods. It is a grove with a sort of an altar in the middle. Round it are the statues of the seven Saxon Gods, from whom we take the names of our days. *[The diarist made a rough sketch of the 7-seat altar on the opposite page of his journal.]*

At the end of the walk which fronts Boycutts buildings, stands a Pavillion call'd Nelson's Pavillion built by Sir John Vanbrugh. It is open in front and is supported by 2 square Ionick pillars and 2 pillasters. The inside is painted al Fresco with 2 storys taken from Bas relieves at the Capitol at Rome; on each side is painted a Vase in Fresco, and under them the 2 following inscriptions alluding to the painting. Under that on the right hand

> Ultra Euphratem, et Tigrim
> usque ad Oceanum propagata ditione
> Orbis terrarum imperium Romae adsignat
> optimus Princeps
> cui super ardua Victoria
> Laurigerum sertum hinc inde
> Utraque manu extendens
> comitantibus Pietate, et abundanta in Capitolio

Under that on the left

> Post obitum L. Veri
> in imperio cum Marco consortis
> Roma integram orbis terrarum
> Potestatem ei, et in eo contulit

At a little distance at the head of a canal stands an Equestrian statue in lead of K: George the 1st made by one Nost with this inscription on the pedestal

> In medio mihi Caesar erit.   Virgil

From hence we pass'd thro' the Parterre close to the house, and on the right hand saw a Dorick arch with a square Pillaster, and round Pillar on each side, fluted, built by Sir John

Vanbrugh; thence we went thro' the orangery, to the Sun-Dial parlour, a green circle with a sun dial in the middle.

From thence passing by the Church we went on to what is call'd the Elysian fields situated in that pt of the garden, which was lately enclos'd. In it is a building by Kent call'd the Mausoleum. It is semicircular. In the middle are the following verses

Hic manus ob patriam pugnando vulnera passi
Quique Pii vates aut Phoebo digna locuti
Inventas aut qui vitam excoluere per artes;
Quique sui memores alios fecere merendo.

Over this inscription is a little sort of a Pyramid, in which in a nich is the head of Mercury with this inscription

Campos ducit ad Elysios

On each side of the building are 8 niches in which are placed, the busts of the worthys. The following ones are there: Q. Elizabeth, Bacon, Shakespear, Inigo Jones, Hampden, K. William, Locke, Sir Isaac Newton, and Milton. Behind this building is a nich in which is the following inscription:

[A half-page is left blank.]

We came next to a little square room irregularly built, with the doors made uneven and little windows. It is call'd the witch house. The inside is painted with odd representations of witches by one Thomas Ferrand a servant of Lord Cobhams.

Beyond this in a grove stands a Corinthian pillar 30 feet high, with a statue of K. George the II upon it. On the plint is wrote

Georgio Augusto.

A little further is an open Rotunda supported by ten Ionick pillars. In the middle of it upon a round pedestal of a blackish Warwickshire Marble stands a gilt statue of Venus de Medicis. This Rotunda fronts a pond, at the upper end of which is a statue of Q. Caroline by four fluted Ionick pillars with their entablature. On each side are three statues of sheperds and sheperdesses dancing.

From hence thro' shady walks we were conducted to the sleeping house, a square room with a double front, a door, and

2 windows in each, with a triangular Pediment supported by 4 Ionick square fluted Pillars. The inside is painted al Fresco with medals hanging by festoons, and Busts over them. On one side is this inscription

Cum omnia sint in incerto, fave tibi.

The last building that we saw was a little sort of an alcove call'd the Randibus, from an affair that happen'd in that place to Mr Rand, the late Minister of the parish. Thereby hangs a tale. Having thus satisfy'd our curiosity at Lord Cobhams gardens we return'd to our Inn, and about 3 in the afternoon, we went on 8 miles to Towcester; the road is mostly thro' Whittlebury forest, and you pass by the little village, that is calld Whittlebury. About half way between Stow and Towcester you enter Northamptonshire.

(BL Add. MS 15776, ff. 2-10)

Anonymous

This manuscript description of the gardens comes from the Stowe Collection at the Huntington Library in California, where it was discovered among the family papers which left Stowe after the 1921 sale. The author is not known. Its twenty-two quarto pages are written in a clear, regular hand, almost without blemish, and stitched together into a booklet, on whose title page are the words "Lord Cobhams Gardens 1738". It must be a special copy, perhaps put together some years after it was written to be presented to a member of the Grenville family.

But however the booklet reached Stowe, its author cannot himself have been a close friend of the family nor a relative. Applying at the gate, he was let into the gardens by the member of the garden staff on duty and then guided round the usual tourist route without ever entering the house. He was an educated, observant man, who commented on things not noticed by others, and in spite of the heavy-footed, jocular tone he adopted from time to time, his account is a very readable one. Especially interesting is his description of the Elysian Fields and the rococo decoration on several of the buildings there, which no one else referred to in such detail. As he realised, it was too fragile to last for more than a few years. Unaccountably he omitted Newton from his list of the British Worthies.

Internal evidence confirms that 1738 was indeed the date of his visit, and it is useful to know that by July of that year Stowe Castle and the Chinese House had both been completed, and that the Palladian Bridge was actually under construction. The description of this independent and informative visitor seems not to have been known to any of the other eighteenth-century writers on Stowe.

Lord Cobhams Gardens 1738

The Entrance into the Gardens is at the End of a long but Narrow Visto, leading up to the front of the House. On Each side of it are Two Portico's of Stone on Ionick Pillars. A Bell hanging on the Wall of the Garden being rung, the Gardiner who attends on Purpose conducts you up a little Ascent till you arrive on the Platform of it.

Opposite this Approach is an Octagon Bason of Water, 400 feet by 300. In the Centre of it is a Rustick Obelisk 60 feet high from the Water's Edge; it was originally designd to have formd a Jettau from the Top of it, and to have fell in a Continual Sheet of Water into the Bason below it, but for want of a due Supply of Water, this Intention cou'd not be put in Practice.

Below this Peice of Water, on the left hand is another of a Long Irregular Form, Containing about Ten acres of Water, and is fed from the Bason above, from whence also is form'd a Cascade which running under the Ground falls down into this Pond through several artificial Craggs and Rocks, plentifully enough for about 2 hours, if required, but for want of a more Vigorous Stream of Water above is at an End till the Reservoir is again replenish'd. At the Head of this Lake (as it is call'd) is a Ruin representing the Remains of Three Stone Arches, with other ruinous Fragments, that are to seem as former Parts of the Ruin.

From hence you are led into a Wilderness of Forest Wood and ever Greens intermixd, wherein is a Cold Bath, more Salubrious I beleive to the Body than pleasant to the Eye; nor is the Wilderness the neatest of it's Kind, but may Justly pass for a Foil to the more delightfull Scenes that afterwards entertain the Eye.

At the End of this Wilderness, on a Small Grass Lawn is built a Summer Retirement call'd the Hermitage which looks down on the Lake aforementiond. The Inside is entirely plain and without farther Ornament than a Small Projection of Arches on the Walls; the outside is very well executed according to the Intention of it, and is designd to appear as Antique, which Tast is very well preserved in the Structure of it.

Leaving this you enter on a Noble Terras of Grass and Gravel, which from hence runs round the whole Gardens, affording many delightfull Views in the Course of it. It Begins from a Semicircular Parterre, in the Centre of which is the Statue of Cain slaying Abel in Lead, and in the middle of the Outline or Verge, stands, fronting the Lower end of the Lake, the Temple of Venus, designd by Mr Kent; two Wings or Colonades supported on Ionick Pillars form the Sides of it, and finish off in 2 little Square Rustick Buildings of three Arches each. On each Side of the Entrance into the Temple are Antique Bustos in Marble of Cleopatra, and Nero, Faustina and Vespasian. The Inside is painted by Slaughter, but is nothing vastly Exquisite. The 2 largest Pannels are Venus dancing with a Company of Satyrs in One, and in the other the same Deity (awake) surrounded by the same Company, all asleep as if wearied either with Dancing, or some other Divertion She had entertaind them with.

One Side of the Temple is furnishd with altars suitable to the Deity of the Place, viz Couches and Pillows; and though the whole Room within is not more than 20 feet Square, it is nevertheless Large enough for the Performance of many Sacrifices.

From this Grand Terras branch out several smaller Walks of Grass and Gravel enclosed with Cutt hedges at the Corners of which are placed various Busts (on Pedestals) of different forms, after the manner of the Terminus's of the Antient. From hence you are led to a Building calld the Belvidere, from the many agreable Prospects that are viewd from it over the several Parts of the Gardens. Among other's, from this Spot is a View of the Castle, lately erected at a Considerable distance out of the Gardens, and has a fine Effect among the Variety of other Edifices within reach of the Eye, and is nowhere seen to a Better Advantage, than from this Place which is raised on [a] small Hill or Tumulus for that Purpose.

After this you enter a Wilderness in the Centre of which is a Green Lawn with the Representation of Two Roman Boxers, in Lead, by Carpenter, which fronts the Adjacent Feilds, and of which through a Space left in the Forest Work no disagreable Prospect is seen.

Having passd the other Wing of this Wilderness you come to the Roman Pavilion, designd by Mr Gibbs; it is within, 24 feet Square, and without, 32. In four Niches are the Statues of Cicero, Marcus Aurelius, Livia and Faustina in Lead Bronzed; all Copys after antique Originals. Without the Bounds of the Garden is another Pavilion opposite to this, of the same form and Height which with the Iron Gates, Palisades and Peirs, form the Grand Entrance into the Park.

From hence you are led to a large Pyramidal Building of Stone in the manner of the celebrated Egyptian Pyramids; it was designd by Sir John Vanbrugh, and is erected here in Memory of him, agreable to which is an Inscription on the Outside of the Pyramid; within under the Pyramid is a Room, but neither the Body of the Architect, nor of any Person is deposited in it, and a Crime it would be, since there is so fine a View from it, that the Dead should possess a Place which they are Uncapable of enjoying the particular delights of. The Room is near 40 feet square and the Pyramid near 60 feet high from the Basis to the Top. En Passant from hence you come to the statues of Hercules and Antaeus in Lead, scituate on the Terras; which on the Inside encircles a meadow left for Variety within the Limits of the Garden, which Horses of particular favour are allow'd Pasture in; and surely Creatures so Usefull to Mankind may claim a Remembrance in the finest Designs, and certainly Virgil was of the same Opinion who has generously introduced them into the Elysian feilds as Usefull Attendants of their once Mortal Masters.

From this Walk you have a distant View of the Temple of Fame, which shall be mentiond in its proper Place. There is scarce a Walk or Lawn in this terrestrial Paradise but is terminated by some Obelisque, Temple, or Mausoleum, and among the rest it would have been a great neglect to have omitted the Respect due to the God of Wine, whose Temple now appears. From the Front of it is a fine Visto of Part of the Lake, an Obelisque, the Meadow and Temple of Venus; the Latter

seems emblematically contrived, since the Votarys of this God
are generally Tributarys to the same Deity, and according to
Terence,

sine Cerere et Baccho friget Venus.

The fabrick is nothing particularly beautyfull, being only of
Rustick Brickwork, and in Sympathy bears the same kind of
Complexion we attribute to it's Jovial Deity. On the Inner Walls
are painted Companys of revelling Bacchanalians, and their
Celestial Patron on the Ceiling with his proper Attendants. The
Painter does not seem to have received any Inspiration from
the God he represented, his Performances being exceedingly
indifferent.

Hence, Passing through one Wing of a Wilderness, you cross
over a long Grass Walk (facing part of the house) into the other
Wing, in the Centre of which is the Saxon Temple (or rather
Grove) so calld from having the Statues of the Deitys revered
by the Old Saxons, placed in it, viz, Sol, Luna, Tubesco, Woden,
Thor, Friga, Saturnus, which were respectively worshipped
on their particular Days of the Week.

This Temple is a Circular Plantation and in the outline of it,
within, is placed the Seven Images abovenamed, and in the
Centre of the Circle is a Large Stone Altar with seven niches
in it for the Preists to officiate in to the Deity of each Day.
Whither this form of the altar is imaginary, or whither the
True representation of their Antient Altar, I dont pretend to
determine, but if the latter, sure the Saxons were very little
addicted to Ceremony and imagined these Hebdomedal
Deitys to be no nice Eaters, since they presumed to feed them
All in so Slovenly a Manner off of one Trencher.

Leaving this Rural Temple you enter on a large Gravel
Walk; at the Upper end of it is a Stone Portico calld the
Roman Temple. The Ceiling within is coved up to the Front
Cornish, and painted with the Figures of Severus presenting
the Globe of the World to the Statue of Rome, attended by
the figures of Fame, Power, Victory, etc. with other designs in
Stone Colours. The Termination of the view from hence
down the Walk is One of the Pavilions at the Entrance into
the Park. The Disposition of these Gardens is so excellent that

Nelson's Seat

Page 17

Saxon Temple

Bickham dee.? to Oct.1750

Engraving by George Bickham
from *The Beauties of Stow*

One and the same Temple Obelisque etc. frequently forms the Termination of many different Views.

From this Walk you pass through another and come to the House. In the Front of it is a large Parterre surrounded by a Ewe hedge, cutt into Niches and Pilasters of various forms, Several Statues, particularly those of the nine Muses, and Urns, being interspersed among them. Down the Centre of the Parterre is a Gravel Walk, leading from the House directly to the entrance into the Gardens, overlooking the Obelisque and Bason before mentioned, and affording a View into the Country upwards of Ten miles. The only Fault it is liable to, is the Narrowness of this Visto, which in respect to the Length, is under a due Wedth.

On one side of this Parterre is the entrance into the Sunn Dial Parlour, so calld from a Sun Dial in the middle of it; it is nothing more than [a] round Plot of about 54 feet in Diameter, encompassd with an Evergreen hedge cut into usual forms. Though this place enjoys the Title of the Sun Dial Parlour I apprehend (from the Closeness of it, being so encircled with Plantations) that the Planet it is dedicated to seldom makes a longer Visit, than just peeping in at the Door.

Having taken Leave of it (which considering Phoebus seldom gives you leave to correct your Watch by his Interpreter here) you may soon do, you walk into a little Elm Grove where is erected a Corinthian Pillar of 30 foot high, and on the Top of it the Statue of his present Majesty; I could but wonder that the Noble Proprietor of this Place should place the Image of what is calld generally Sacred Majesty among so many Temples, Deitys and Persons of Heathen reputation as we had lately passd by.

From hence you go into a Wilderness, in which is a small Building open in Front like an Alcove, Call'd Dido's Cave, the Story of Æneas and that Queen being painted on the Wall. It has been reported that this has been the Scene of more Modern Amours; and as the Antient Hero of the first Story is said to have been of Divine Race, the later one according to Fame was of Divine Profession. This memorable Ædifice is seated on an Amphitheatre of Grass, cutt into Slopes and shaded with Covert proper for the Use that they say has been made of it.

Going from hence you walk down a Gravel Walk till you arrive at the Rotundo; it stands on ten Ionick Pillars, and the Statue of Venus de Medicis is in the middle within; the Roof being a Dome Supported by the Pillars abovenamed. The Diameter (within the steps you ascend by) is about 24 feet. From hence is an Extensive View of the Gardens, and among other objects at a small distance off is the Statue of the late Queen (on a Colum) supported by Four Pillars; it stands in a mixture of Lawrels and ever Greens, several Statues (but none Curious) being quarterd in niches of the Forest Work, which outline a pretty green Lawn with an oblong Canal running down the middle Division of it. This Part is calld the Queen's Theatre.

You again go into a Wilderness where at the end of a Grass Walk is a Room calld the Sleeping Parlour, and as it is furnishd with Easy Chairs and Couches, I must confess it to be very Proper for the Purpose.

From this Wilderness you cross over the Walk leading up to the House into another Wilderness, in which is an odd Sort of a Building calld the Witch House. The Walls within are daub'd over with Scenes of an Old Witch and her Performances, drawn by a Domestick of Lord Cobhams; but in such a manner, that though the Painter himself could make a Woman a Witch, he plainly proves himself to have been no Conjurer.

This is the last Thing of observation in the Old Gardens.

The New Gardens

The admission into these is through a small Wilderness, up to the Temple of Fame. On One Side of it is a Ruin, much exceeding that at the Head of the Lake, not only in Size but Execution. The Temple is a Circular Building ascended to by 12 Steps in the front; round it are 16 Pillars which support the Frize and Dome; within it is entirely plain, except 4 Niches in the Wall with the Statues of Homer, Epaminondas, Lycurgus and Socrates; the Diameter within is about 20 feet. From the front the Eye commands the Mausoleum (of which hereafter) the Serpentine River, the Castle, etc.

Walking through another Wilderness, you come to the Shell Rotundo, scituate at the head of a little Rill of Water, which from hence runs through the Wilderness. The Work and Contrivance of it is vastly Curious in its Kind; and having hitherto visited only Temples of Brick and Stone, the Entertainment and Surprise is the greater on the unexpected Appearance of so Uncommon a Structure. The Roof is a Dome coverd with the Shells of large Tortoises intermixd with small ones that close the Joints and Vacuitys; the Cornice and Frize is a good Proportionate Depth, and I may say (for Regularity) strung round with many Rows of little shells of different kinds; the Columns that support it are Serpentine, crusted over with Variety of Shells of beautyfull Colours, stuck on with great Nicety and exactness: but the Inside of the Dome requires the most Admiration, the Ceiling being divided into as many Quarters as there are Pillars that sustain it, in each of which is a humane Face (in Grotesque Character) exactly painted in different colourd shells on a Ground of the same kind of Materials. Beautys are of short Continuance in general, and it is to be fear'd this will prove too tender to resist the force of Winds and Weather; should it fall a Victim to the Rage of Mercyless Tempests the Less will be the Concern, since the Designer and Lord of it is as expeditious in Building as ever was Amphion, the Fortune of the one supplying him with as much Capacity as the harp did the other.

Part of the Garden beyond this is as yet unfinish'd, though the Design is in Execution. In the middle of an old Pond (which is to be enlarged) is a house built on piles, after the manner of the Chinese, odd and Pretty enough, but as the form of their Building is so well known from Prints and other Descriptions, there is no Occasion to say more of it.

Most Part of this new Garden is called the Elyzian Feilds; and the Way to the Church is designd to be through some Part of them, from which one Inconvenience may arise, viz that unless the Influence of the Preacher is great indeed, More will pay there Devotions among the Antient Heathens than the Modern Xtians; it is to be confess'd (if we Credit History as Evidence for the Former, and our own Eyes as Judges of the latter) many of the more antient Gentlemen were Persons of the greater Merit.

A little farther on is a Bridge of rough Stone designd in a Ruinous manner. From under it runs a Serpentine River of a good Breadth; the Ground on each side gradually ascending and well laid down, with the Forest Work that crowns the Banks a Top, make this as agreable to my Eye as any Part of the Gardens. On one side of this River on the Top of the Slope is the Mausoleum, fronting the Water, of which we have before had a View from the Temple of Fame. This Building is the Segment of a Large Circle and in the Elevation of it are niches filld with Busts, carved in Stone; the first is, of Mr Pope, the 2d Lord Bacon, 3d Milton, 4th Inigo Jones, 5th Shakespear, 6th Lock, 7th John Hamden Esq., 8th King Alfred, 9th Queen Elizabeth, 10th Edward Prince of Wales, 11th King William 3d, 12th Sir Walter Raleigh, 13th Sir Francis Drake, 14th Sir Thomas Gresham, the 15th and last, Sir John Barnard. In a Pediment Nich in the middle over these Busto's is, that of Mercury with this Motto, Campos ducit ad Elysios. On the Back of this Building is a little Cell, where is buried a once Favourite Greyhound, and on the Wall is an Inscription of some Length to the Memory of him and enumerating his many good Qualitys; the Substance is, that he was a sincere and faithful Companion, Father of a large Offspring, not in the least Unworthy of so good a Parent, that he was no Atheist, though he believed none of the 39 Articles, etc. with many other Expressions, that deceive the Reader till he comes to the last Line, Wonder not, Reader, at his so great Virtues (or Words Tantamount) for he was not a Man but a Greyhound. A good Burlesque on human Panegyrick.

After a short Walk along the Banks of the Serpentine River, you cross over it by a Bridge into the other Division of the Elyzian feilds, where the first Thing that invites the Eye is Congreves Monument; the Design is Pyramidal, embelish'd with the Figures of Satyrs, a Monkey and other Emblematical Designs. This Memorial stands on the side of a Gravel Terras, which on the Left encloses another Green Meadow for Pasture, Larger, than that before mention'd.

The Gravel Walk leads you from hence to a magnificent Bridge, now building, in order to make a Passage over the Serpentine River into the 3d Division of these New Gardens, which at present is no farther Executed than a Bare Design and choice of Ground for the Purpose. The Bridge consists of one large Arch, with a Smaller on each side of it; the Piers and Butments are Rustick from the Water's Edge to a Proper Height above the Crown of the Arches, and from thence the Work is carryd up with Windows, Balconies, etc. ornamented with Festoons, and other Peices of Carved Work and the whole is roof'd over from Side to Side, so that this Peice of Architecture not only carrys you over the Water, but if a Sudden Shower interrupts your Walk you here find a Shelter from the Water above you. A good Bridge that not only carrys one safe over, but also dry, under the Water. The Scaffolds and Men employ'd on this Work prevented a perfect View of it. Returning from the Bridge you are not led back by the Way of the Terras, but walk up to a Large Gravel Walk in the Margin of the Garden, in the same Manner as the Great Terras in [the] Old Gardens; at this End of the Walk are a large Set of Iron Gates, whence, by the Removal of some Ordinary Buildings a View is to be open'd into the Country. Here stands the Statue of the Roman Gladiator fronting up the Walk, and from hence you go along the Walk till you come to the Steps you first enterd at, having now, together with the outline and Cross Walks, paced better than Three Miles and a half, Ground enough, to make your Stomach by this Time, as much Impatient to eat, as your Eye before was to see.

(Huntington Library, Stowe Temple Manorial Papers, Box 8)

Page 58

Congreve's Monument

um according to Act 1750.

Engraving by George Bickham
from *The Beauties of Stow*

Daniel Defoe (c.1660 – 1731)
and Samuel Richardson (1689 – 1761)

This famous travel book published by Defoe in 1724 was reprinted eight times in the next half century, being revised and enlarged by its successive editors. Samuel Richardson, the novelist, was responsible for the third edition, which came out in 1742 and was noteworthy for its lengthy appendix. The greater part of this was taken up by the accounts of six gardens, which were described there in detail for the first time, with a note that it was intended they should "be incorporated in their proper Places, in future Editions of this Work."

Of the thirty-two pages no fewer than seventeen (pages 271-287) were devoted to Stowe, indicating the fame which the gardens had already gained among the touring public, and when Seeley adopted the description two years later as the basis of his own pioneering guidebook, it became the source of the long line of Stowe guides. Some re-arrangement was necessary to bring it into a sequence which followed the visitor's normal circuit of the gardens, and it included a number of errors which had to be corrected later. But, even so, it remains a key document.

from *A Tour thro' the Whole Island
of Great Britain*
Appendix to the third edition (1742)

We enter'd on the South-side of the Garden, between Two square
Pavilions of the *Dorick* Order, the Work of Sir *John Vanbrugh*; and
were struck with the surprising Grandeur and Variety of the
Objects that presented themselves to our View, of which I shall
give a brief Account in Order, as we passed them.

First, then, in the Middle of a large Octagon Piece of Water,
stands an Obelisk of near 70 Feet, which is design'd for a *Jet-d'Eau*
to cascade from the Top of it. At a good Distance we beheld
Two beautiful Rivers, which join, and enter the Octagon in
One Stream. Over One of the Rivers is a *Palladian* Bridge, which
is an agreeable Object. A *Gothick* Building, 70 Feet high,
presents itself on the Summit of a fine Hill; which, we were
told, is intended to be dedicated to *Liberty.*

Here we had likewise a View of the South Front of the House,
up an Avenue of stately Trees; but great Objections have been
made to the Narrowness of it, which is, no doubt, an essential
Fault. However, since every Tree may be deem'd a sort of Obelisk
to the Honour of the noble Planter, it makes a good Excuse for
their standing; and the rather, as, if they were taken away, it
would create an Evil, which could not be remedied in 40 Years.

As the *Gothick* Building is on the Right-hand, so on the Left
appears an *Egyptian* Pyramid, dedicated to the Memory of
Sir *John Vanbrugh.*

In short, here is such a Scene of Magnificence and Nature
display'd, the Fields abounding with Cattle, the Trees and
Water so delightfully intermingled, and such a charming
Verdure, Symmetry, and Proportion, every-where presenting
to the Eye, that the Judgment is agreeably puzzled, which
singly to prefer of so many collected Beauties.

Leaving this Point, and on the Left-hand passing by Three
Statues, we came to the Cold-bath, from whence we beheld a
natural Cascade falling down from the before-mentioned
Octagon, in Three different Sheets of Water, into a large Lake.

Engraving by George Bickham from *The Beauties of Stow*

One of the Sheets glides thro' an Arch, or Piece of Ruin, which is mostly hid by a Clump of Ever-greens; but his Lordship, as we are told, designs to make a good deal of Amendment to it, tho' at present it has a very natural and agreeable Appearance.

From hence we proceeded to the Hermitage, which is agreeably situated in a rising Wood, and by the Side of the Lake; and passing thro' the Wood, we came to the Statues of *Cain* and *Abel*, fronting the *Veneris Hortus*, a very neat Structure, designed by Mr. *Kent*, the Inside of it painted by Mr. *Sleats*; and on the Frize is the following Motto, alluding to the Painting in the Cave:

"Nunc amet, qui nondum amavit;
Quique amavit, nunc amet."

Which is,

"He who ne'er lov'd, a Lover grow;
And he who has—continue so."

Here is likewise a *Sophia*. Each Way, from the Entrance of the Room, is a handsome Colonnade, leading to square Tabernacles or Pavilions. Here are also Four venerable antique Bustoes, of *Vespasian*, *Nero*, *Cleopatra*, and *Faustina*.

Hence to the Head of the Lake we had a pleasant View of the Cascade; and from hence to *Gibbs's* Building, or the *Belvidere*, which is placed on the Top of the Mount, is a noble Prospect of the House, the Church, the Effigies of his present Majesty, and the late Queen; the Rotonda; the Castle, which a Farmer now inhabits, and was built for that Purpose; but on account of its being seated on the Side of a fine rising Hill, makes a beautiful Appearance as well from hence, as from many other Places.

In the Garden is likewise the Temple of *Friendship*, from which the Pavilion at the Entrance, the Cascade, the Lake, one of the Fields that is inclosed in the Garden, all together afford a Scene truly charming.

From hence to *Boycoat* Buildings, passing thro' a pleasant Wood with several agreeable Prospects into the Country, we saw on our Right-hand a noble Terrace. One of the Buildings is a very good habitable House; the other stands on a square

Bottom in the Garden; and in the Inside of it are Four Statues, at full Length, in Niches; viz. *Cicero, Faustina, Marcus Aurelius,* and *Livia.* The Buildings are both finish'd with pyramidical Tops, by *Gibbs.* Betwixt them is a very handsome Gate-way, which is the second Entrance to the House, from which leads up a noble Avenue, planted with double Lines of thriving Trees.

From hence to the *Egyptian* Pyrāmid mentioned before, which is 60 Feet high, and about half Way up, is this Inscription in very large Characters:

"Inter plurima hortorum horum ædificia a JOHANNE VANBRUGH, equite, designata, hanc pyramidem illius memoriæ sacram esse voluit COBHAM."

In *English* thus:

"Among a very great Number of Structures in these Gardens, designed by Sir JOHN VANBRUGH, Knight, COBHAM thought fit, that this Pyramid should be sacred to his Memory."

And in the Inside of the Building is the following Inscription:

"Lusisti satis, edisti satis, atque bibisti: Tempus abire tibi est; ne potum largius æquo Rideat & pulset lasciva decentius ætas."

Which may be thus translated:

"Enough you've sported, quaff'd the Bowl, and eat: 'Tis Time that from the Banquet you retreat; Lest Youth, more fitly frolicksome, may join To push you, reeling under Loads of Wine."

From hence going along a sort of Fortification Walk on our Left-hand, the Wood on the other Hand, we enter'd the Field, which is inclosed in a military Way, with a staked Fence. At the first Angle, on the middle of the Gravel-walk, are the Statues of *Hercules* and *Antëus.* Hence we proceeded to *St. Augustine's* Cave, which is a Building of Roots of Trees and Moss; and in it a Straw Couch with Three Inscriptions in *Monkish Latin* Verse. It is placed in a natural Wood, and from the Oddness of the

Fabrick, and the agreeable Simplicity which is round it, makes a very entertaining Variety.

Leaving this Place, we approached a Building of a very different Nature—the Temple of *Bacchus,* built of Brick, with Paintings in the Inside alluding to the Name. Here we had a fine distant Prospect toward *Aylesbury* and *Wendover* Hills, etc. In the Garden we had in full View the Temple of *Venus:* and between the Two is an Obelisk erected to the Memory of a Clergyman, with this Inscription:

To the Memory of ROBIN COUCHER.

We proceeded from hence to the *Saxon* Temple, which is a solemn Grove with the Seven *Saxon* Deities presiding over the several Days of the Week, placed in Niches; and in the Middle of them stands an Altar, as for Sacrifice. All the Statues are extremely good, and this Scene agreeably strikes the Mind with Serenity and Composure.

Our Eye, after being confined in the Wood, breaking at once out of it, we were surprised with a fine open Country on the North: on the South, the Rotonda appears: on the West, the *Boycoat* Buildings: on the East, the Equestrian Statue of the late King, which stands in the Front of the House. These Objects present themselves from *Nelson's* Seat, which is an oblong square Recess in a Clump of Ever-greens. To the South-east is a View of the Mansion-house, which is an extraordinary good one; but, his Lordship annually adding to and improving it, one may safely say, that it will not be much inferior to the best House in *England,* if his Lordship's Design is finished.

The Offices on the North-side are all inclosed within a most elegant Wall, with Niches, and grand Gate-ways into the Offices and Gardens. The House and Offices, when perfected, will be about 640 Feet in Length, fronting North and South. As *Nelson's* Seat lies to the North-west from the Portico of the House, there is on the North-east a new Bastion building to answer it; and some grand Walks are now making by the Side of a fine Lawn, from which we see numerous Herds of Deer. A Semicircle of fine Timber appears at some Miles Distance with an agreeable country between.

On the South Front of the House is a very handsome Parterre, decorated with *Apollo* and the Muses, gilt Vessels, and Two Orangeries: but it is likely this will be intirely altered; for if the lower End is laid open, there will appear a noble Scene, where Nature and Art are curiously blended.

The next Object of our View was a *Corinthian* Column, on which is the Statue of his present Majesty, with this Inscription:

GEORGIO AVGUSTO.

Here we had a most delightful Prospect over the Country; and in the Garden several of the Buildings present themselves with great Pomp. The Lake, whose Bounds are beautifully concealed, adds much to the general Agreeableness of the Place.

Dido's Cave was the next Subject of our Attention: this is a Stone Building, in a Wood, and raised on a sort of Amphitheatre, with this Inscription:

"Speluncam *Dido*, dux & *Trojanus*, eandem
Deveniunt…"

In *English* thus:

"Repairing to the same dark Cave are seen,
The *Trojan* Hero, and the *Tyrian* Queen."

From hence we advanced to the Rotonda, which is a neat airy Building by Sir *John Vanbrugh*. The Dome of it supported on Ten *Dorick* Columns; and in the Centre, standing on a circular Pedestal, a *Venus à Medicis*. From this Place we had a View of Part of the Octagon; the Lake, the Fields, and several of the Buildings, presenting themselves alternately as we turned ourselves round.

As we went from hence to the late Queen's Statue, by the Side of a Canal, we were delighted with an Alteration of his Lordship's; *viz*. On each Side the Ground is broken, and planted with Clumps of various kinds of Trees, intermixt with Statues, which are promiscuously placed. Her late Majesty's

Effigies is erected on Four *Ionick* Columns, which are placed on a large Pedestal, with this Inscription in Golden Letters:

"Honori, Laudi, Virtuti Divæ CAROLINÆ."

"To the Honour, Praise, and Virtue of the Divine CAROLINE."

It is situated on a neat Amphitheatre of Slopes, with pastoral Figures each Way from it. Nature and Art here, joining together, make an agreeable Contraste.

Next we were led into the Sleeping Parlour, which is a square Building placed in a Wood with Six Walks centring in it. Within, are painted the *Cæsars* Heads, with several Festons of Fruit, etc. On the Frize is this Inscription:

"Cum omnia sint in incerto, fave tibi."

Which is,

"Since all Things are uncertain, indulge thyself."

Leaving this Place, and crossing the Avenue before-mentioned, from the Pavilions we came to the Witch-house, a square Building, the Inside of which is painted by my Lord's Gentleman, with several Devices alluding to the Name.

We arrived next at the Temple of *Antient Virtue*, a Rotonda of the *Dorick* Order, by Mr. *Kent:* and in Four Niches, standing at full Lengths, are the Four following Statues; *viz.*

I. EPAMINONDAS, with this Inscription over his Head:

"Cujus a virtute, prudentia, verecundia,
Thebanorum respublica
Libertatem simul & imperium,
Disciplinam bellicam, civilem & domesticam,
Accepit;
Eoque amisso, perdidit."

That is,

"From whose Valour, Prudence, and Moderation, the Republick of *Thebes* received both Liberty and Empire, its military, civil, and domestick Discipline; and, with him, lost them."

II. LYCURGUS, with this:

"Qui summo cum consilio inventis legibus,
Omnemque contra corruptelam munitis optime,
Pater patriæ,
Libertatem firmissimam,
Et mores sanctissimos,
Expulsa cum divitiis avaritia, luxuria, libidine,
In multa secula
Civibus suis instituit."

Thus translated:

"Who having invented Laws with the greatest Wisdom, and most excellently fenced them against all Corruption, as a Father of his Country, instituted for his Countrymen the firmest Liberty, and the soundest Morality, which endured for many Ages, he having, together with Riches, banished Avarice, Luxury, and Lust."

III. SOCRATES,

"Qui corruptissima in civitate innocens,
Bonorum hortator, unici cultor DEI,
Ab inutili otio, & vanis disputationibus,
Ad officia vitæ, & societatis commoda,
Philosophiam avocavit,
Hominum sapientissimus."

That is,

"Who being innocent in a most corrupt State, an Encourager of the Good, a Worshipper of One only GOD, as the wisest of Men, reduced Philosophy from useless Indolence, and vain Disputations, to the Duties of Life, and the Advantages of Society."

IV. HOMERUS,

"Qui poetarum princeps, idem & maximus,
Virtutis præco, & immortalitatis largitor,
Divino carmine,
Ad pulcre audendum, & patiendum fortiter,
Omnibus notus gentibus, omnes incitat."

Thus rendered:

"Who being the First of Poets, as he was the greatest, the Herald of Virtue, and Bestower of Immortality, known to all Nations, incites all, in a Divine Poem, honourably to dare, and resolutely to suffer."

Over one Door is this Inscription:

"Charum esse civem, bene de republica mereri, laudari, coli, diligi, gloriosum est: metui vero, & in odio esse, invidiosum, detestabile, imbecillum, caducum."

Which is:

"To be dear to our Country, to deserve well of the State, to be praised, honoured, and beloved, is glorious: but to be dreaded, and hated, is matter of Ill-will, detestable, weak, ruinous."

Over the other Door this:

"Justitiam cole & pietatem, quæ cum sit magna in parentibus & propinquis, tum in patria maxima est. Ea vita via est in cœlum, & in hunc cœtum eorum, qui jam vixerunt."

In *English* thus:

"Maintain Justice, and thy relative Duty; which, as it is great, when exercised toward our Parents and Kindred, so is greatest toward our Country. That Life is the Way to Heaven, and to this Assembly of those, who have already lived."

From this Place we had no distant Prospect, but, notwithstanding that, it abounds with lasting Beauties: it is really placed in a sort of Paradise; and, Things rising adequate to that Name, you see *Friendship* flourishing in immortal Youth; in the *Elysian Fields* are many great and virtuous Mens Names perpetuated, who have distinguished themselves in *this* World by answering the End of their Creation. Near this Place also is a good Emblem of those who have deviated from it, in the Ruin. Here are sweet purling Streams, resembling the melodious Sounds of Birds, etc.

We were now not far from the Parish Church, which is so closely surrounded with a Wood, as not to be seen. From hence we came to the Side of a River, where

> "Unpolish'd Nature cannot boast a Part;
> For Chance too regular, too rude for Art."

And by its winding Banks we were led up to a Grotto, which is to be decorated with Shells, Pebbles, and Minerals. Here is likewise a Shell-pavilion, the Dome of which is supported by Six wreathed Columns. The Inside of it hath several Marks performed from Shells, and divers other Imbellishments. On the opposite Side is to be another of Pebbles.

Hence we proceeded to the Three-arch'd Building, which is a pleasant Recess, by the Banks of the River; and in passing we saw *Antient Virtue* peeping on the South-side of us. The Church we had in full View on the West. To the East is situated the *Chinese* House, a Building in the Pond, the Out-side of it painted very ingeniously, in the *Chinese* Taste, by the celebrated Mr. *Sleats*. The Inside of it is *Indian* Japan.

The Shell Bridge led us from hence into the *Elysian Fields*, the most charming Place that ever Eyes beheld. It may not be improper here to give the following Lines, which were left by an unknown Gentleman, on his Entrance into them:

To Lord COBHAM.

> "Charm'd with the Sight, my ravish'd Breast is fir'd
> With Hints like those, which antient Bards inspir'd.
> All the feign'd Tales, by Superstition told,
> All the bright Train of fabled Nymphs of old,
> Th' enthusiastick Muse believes, are true;
> Thinks the Spot sacred, and its Genius You.
> Lost in wild Rapture, would she fain disclose,
> How by Degrees the pleasing Wonder rose,
> Industrious in a faithful Verse to trace
> The various Beauties of the lovely Place;
> And while she keeps the glowing Work in View,
> Thro' ev'ry Maze your artful Hand pursue," *&c.*

We are now come to the Monuments of *British* Worthies; the First of which is Mr. POPE, with no Inscription.

The next is Sir THOMAS GRESHAM, with this Inscription:

"Who, by the honourable Profession of Merchant, having enriched himself, and his Country; for carrying on the Commerce of the World, built the ROYAL EXCHANGE."

INIGO JONES,

"Who, to adorn his Country, introduced and rivalled the *Greek* and *Roman* Architecture."

JOHN MILTON,

"Whose sublime and unbounded Genius equalled a Subject that carried him beyond the Limits of this World."

WILLIAM SHAKESPEARE,

"Whose excellent Genius opened to him the whole Heart of Man, all the Stores of Nature; and gave him Power, beyond all other Writers, to move, astonish, and delight Mankind."

SIR ISAAC NEWTON,

"Whom the GOD of Nature made to comprehend all his Works; and from simple Principles to discover the Laws never known, and to explain the Appearances never understood, of this stupendous Universe."

Sir FRANCIS BACON, Lord VERULAM,

"Who, by the Strength of a superior Genius, rejecting vain Speculation, and fallacious Theory, taught to pursue and improve Philosophy by the certain Method of Experiment."

In the Niche of a Pyramid is placed a *Mercury*, with these Words subscribed:

"...CAMPOS DUCIT AD ELYSIOS."

"...Leads to th' *Elysian* Fields."

And below this Figure is fix'd a Square of black Marble, with the following Lines:

"Hic manus ob patriam pugnando vulnera passi,
Quique pii vates, & Phœbo digna locuti,
Inventas aut qui vitam excoluere per artes,
Quique sui memores alios fecere merendo."

Thus translated:

"Here are the Bands, who for their Country bled;
And Bards whose pure and sacred Verse is read:
Those who, by Arts invented, Life improv'd;
And by their Merits made their Mem'ries lov'd."

King ALFRED,

"The mildest, justest, most beneficent of Kings, who drove out the *Danes,* secured the Seas, supported Learning, established Juries, crush'd Corruption, guarded Liberty, and was the Founder of the *English* Constitution."

EDWARD Prince of *Wales,*

"The Terror of *Europe,* and Delight of *England*; who preserved unaltered, in the Height of Glory, his natural Gentleness and Modesty."

Queen ELIZABETH,

"Who confounded the Projects, and destroyed the Designs of *Spain,* who threatened to oppress the Liberty of *Europe*; took off the Yoke of Ecclesiastical Tyranny; restored Religion from the Corruptions of Popery; and by a wise, a moderate, and a popular Government, gave Wealth, Health, Security to *England.*"

King WILLIAM the Third,

"Who by his Virtue and Constancy having saved his Country from a foreign Master, by a bold and generous Enterprize, preserved the Liberty and Religion of *Great Britain.*"

Sir WALTER RALEGH,

"A valiant Soldier, and an able Statesman; who, endeavouring to rouse the Spirit of his Master, for the Honour of his Country, against the Ambition of *Spain,* fell a Sacrifice to that Court, whose Arms he had vanquished, and whose Designs he had opposed."

Sir FRANCIS DRAKE,

"Who, thro' many Perils, was the First of *Britons,* that adventured to sail round the Globe, and carry into unknown Seas the Knowlege and Glory of the *English* Name."

JOHN HAMPDEN,

"Who with great Spirit and consummate Ability, began a noble Opposition to an arbitrary Court, in Defence of the Liberties of his Country; supported them in Parliament, and died for them in the Field."

Sir JOHN BARNARD,
With no Inscription.

Leaving this incomparably sweet Place with great Regret, as every one who sees it, must, we came to a Monument, with this Inscription:

Signor FIDO,

"An *Italian* of good Extraction, who came into *England,* not to bite us, like most of his Countrymen, but to gain an honourable Livelihood: he hunted not after Fame; yet acquired it: regardless of the Praise of his Friends, but most sensible of their Love. Tho' he lived amongst the Great, he neither learnt nor flattered any Vice. He was no Bigot, nor doubted he of any of the XXXIX. Articles: and if to follow Nature, and respect the Laws of Society, be Philosophy, he was a perfect Philosopher; a faithful Friend, and an agreeable Companion, a loving Husband, and distinguished by a numerous Off-spring, all which he lived to see take good Courses; and in his Old-age retired to the House of a Clergyman in the Country, where he finished his earthly Race, and died an Honour and Example to the whole Species. Reader, this Stone is guiltless of Flattery; for he, to whom it was inscribed, was not a Man, but a ——"

Crossing the Field to the *Gothick* Building before described, we had a boundless Prospect round the Building. From hence we descended a fine Hill; and on our Left-hand saw a Plantation of Ever-greens; on our Right the Well designed *[sic],* and Rivers

described from the Pavilion. This Walk led us down to a very
handsome Bridge over one of the Rivers. The Roof on the Side
facing the Water is supported by *Ionick* Columns; the Backside of it by an *Alto-Relievo* of the Four Quarters of the World,
bringing their Products to *Britannia*. Here are likewise
painted by Mr. *Sleats*, Sir *Walter Ralegh*, with a Map of *Virginia*
in his Hand; and Sir *William Penn*, holding a Book styled *The
Laws of* Pensylvania. Here are, besides, a great many modern
and antique Bustoes of Marble.

We now visited the *Imperial* Closet, which is a Room very
near the Form of a Cube; and in it are the three following
Figures, painted at full Length by Mr. *Sleats:*

IMP. TITUS. CÆS. VESPASIAN.

With his Saying over his Head, *Diem perdidi, I have lost a Day*.

IMP. TRAJAN. CÆS.

With his Saying, *Pro me: si merear, in me. For me: but if I deserve
it, against me*.

IMP. MARCUS. AURELIUS. CÆSAR. ANTONINUS.

With his Saying, *Ita regas imperator, ut privatus regi velis. So
govern when an Emperor, as, if a private Person, you would desire to
be governed*.

Passing a noble Iron Gate, at the End of a fine Terrace, of
1990 Feet in Length, and Breadth proportionable, which leads
to the *Veneris Hortus*, we came to the Temple of *Friendship*, a
lofty square Building, of the *Dorick* Order, with Three noble
Porticoes on the Sides, which appear to the Garden. The Cave
and Ceiling are painted with History-pieces, by Mr. *Sleats*. At
the Bottom of the Room are placed Ten Pedestals, which are
designed for the Bustoes of his Lordship, and Nine of his select
Friends. Those of his Royal Highness the Prince of *Wales*, the
Earl of *Chesterfield*, Lord *Cobham*, and Mr. *William Pitt*, are
already erected; but who the other are to be, is not yet known.

The Pebble Alcove is a neat Recess, and very artfully
imbellished with Pebbles. His Lordship's Arms are performed
with the same, and display'd in proper Colours.

Congreve's Monument is an Urn, which with great Art expresses the Genius of the Man; and at the Top of it is placed a Monkey, beholding himself in a Mirror, and under him this Writing:

Vitæ imitatio,
Consuetudinis speculum,
Comœdia.

That is,

Comedy is the Imitation of Life, and the Glass of Fashion.

The Poet's Effigies, lying in a careless Posture, has the following Inscription:

Ingenio
Acri, faceto, expolito,
Moribusque
Urbanis, candidis, facillimis,
GULIELMI CONGREVE,
Hoc
Qualecunque desiderii sui
Solamen simul &
Monumentum
Posuit COBHAM.
M.DCC.XXXVI.

Thus translated:

In the Year 1736. COBHAM *erected this poor consolation for, as well as Monument of, his Loss of the piercing, elegant, polished Wit, and civilized, candid, most unaffected Manners, of* WILLIAM CONGREVE.

We were now very near the Pavilions, and in going to them, walked by the Side of the River and Octagon, passing, on our Left-hand, Three *Satyrs,* and a *Dancing Venus.*

I have now gone round, giving you a faint Description of an unparalleled Chain of artificial and natural Beauty: and, to make use of Mr. *Pope*'s Lines,

Here Order in Variety you see,
Where all things differ, yet where all agree.

His Lordship's Judgment, and refin'd Taste, are not less conspicuous in his Woods and Park.

Samuel Boyse (1708 – 1749)

In June, July and August of 1742 this poem was printed by instalments in successive numbers of the *Gentleman's Magazine*. Though it was published anonymously, there is general agreement that its author was Samuel Boyse (1708-49), who was brought up in Dublin, the son of a dissenting minister, and moved first to Edinburgh, then to London. He was a competent scholar with some literary skill, but he achieved little of note and was forced, during his latter years, to earn a precarious living writing verses such as these for the literary magazines.

The poem itself is commonplace and inferior to Gilbert West's *Stowe* (1732). More interesting than the text are the footnotes, which make up almost a third of the whole. These indicate that Boyse based his work on the third edition of Defoe's *Tour*, which was published in the same year, using its route round the gardens as the pattern for his own. He supplemented and corrected this with information from other sources, notably from West, whose version he sensibly followed where it differed from the *Tour*. He also seems to have had access to the engraved views of Stowe by Jacques Rigaud, another reliable witness, though he repeated Rigaud's only known error when he described the straight canal on the north side as a round pond full of swans.

These two provided Boyse with a generally accurate picture of the old gardens, the area reached first on the visitor's circuit. So he was speaking more truthfully than he would have cared to admit when he paused, as if awestruck, at the entrance to the Elysian Fields (line 234) and exclaimed,

"But stop my Muse—I feel a conscious fear."

The fact was that he had just reached the limit of the territory described by West and illustrated by Rigaud, and from this point onwards he knew he had to struggle on without their help.

Being a confident classical scholar, Boyse was able to name the authors of the inscriptions quoted in the *Tour*, adding several extra Latin quotations himself in the footnotes, and from his antiquarian reading he introduced Hengist and, inevitably, the Druids into his poem. But there is no evidence that he ever visited the gardens himself. On the contrary, his description has all the appearance of being second-hand. So it is surprising to find a few things in it which are recorded there in print for the first time, most importantly the detailed description of the Chinese House (note 39), which was taken over word for word by Seeley for his guidebook two years later. Granted the second-hand nature of the rest, this passage too is likely to have come from a printed source, perhaps a newspaper, which has yet to be discovered.

The original instalments can be found in Vol XII of the *Gentleman's Magazine*, on pages 324, 380-2 and 435-6. The spelling and capital letters of the poem, but not the italics, follow the text of 1742. Somewhat more freedom has been taken with the style of the notes to make them easier to read.

The Triumphs of Nature

A Poem,
on the magnificent Gardens at Stowe in Buckinghamshire,
the Seat of the Rt. Hon. Lord Cobham.
(1742)

> *Here order in variety you see,*
> *Where all things differ,—yet where all agree!*
>
> Mr. Pope

> *Ut pictura poesis erit.*   Hor.

Delightful Nature!—child of heavenly light!
Whose form inchants us, and whose smiles invite!
Once more, chaste Goddess, animate the song,
Inspire the lays!—to thee the lays belong!
My steps conduct,—be thou my charming Guide
Amidst the scenes that show thy noblest pride;
Where pleas'd, thy hand elysian bow'rs prepares,
To bless the Hero's toils—the Patriot's cares!
    Begin, fond muse!—but whither am I tost?
Where have I stray'd?—in sweet confusion lost!   10
Thee, Goddess, I behold with pleas'd surprize,
Confess'd, like monarchs in a rich disguise!
Thy native majesty attracts the heart,
And shows thy empire o'er the works of Art:
So Virtue shines in Cobham's steddy mind,
And leaves the shadowy forms of pomp behind.

*Here Art attends—and waits thy ruling will,
For she at best is but thy hand-maid still;
If thou thy state imperial wouldst express,
She looks thy wardrobe, and puts on thy dress!   20
In the clear wave the chrystal mirror holds,
Or rich with gems thy flow'ry robe unfolds:
If ornaments thou slight, and pomp displease,
She then retires;—and leaves thee to thy ease:
Leaves thee to take thy evening walk unseen,
O'er the sequester'd shade, or lonesome green;
Where meditation sooths thy thoughtful breast,
And birds and waters lull thee to thy rest:
Where they who never knew thy charms—may know,
For all thy countless charms are seen at Stowe.   30
Two square Pavilions[1] opening to the scene
First lead the Muse to the inchanted plain.
Whence to the north this Tempe we survey,
Its glories brightening to meridian day!
Hence spreads a liquid octagon to view,
And charms the eye with its unclouded blue;
Full in the midst an obelisk[2] ascends,
And high in air the wat'ry column sends;
Two distant rivers winding from the right
Descend[3]—and in one spacious stream unite;   40
Which gently gliding thro' its verdant shores,
In the broad octagon its treasures pours:
High on a summit all below commands,

---

* Thro' this whole scene of variety the improvements are adapted
    to follow the luxuriant fancy of Nature, and humour her
    different propensities; you see her adorn'd and enrich'd where
    necessity or propriety bespeak such indulgence; but in the
    simplicity of her own dress, where art or ornaments would
    disfigure her native beauty. Brit. Trav. Vol. 3. p.120.
1. Two pavilions supported by Doric columns form the south entry
    to the gardens.
2. A large Octagon bason with an Obelisk in the center 70 feet
    high designed for a *Jet d'eau*.
3. Over one of these streams is a Palladian bridge.

Fair Liberty [4] thy destin'd temple stands;
Where, like some queen expell'd her lawful throne,
A refuge thou shalt find—thy value known,
And see lost realms—that once were all thy own!
 North thro' an avenue,[5] the growth of years!
The distant mansion to the eye appears;
Which still transported as it turns around,   50
Beholds new charms diversify the ground;
Here numerous herds that range th' adjacent plain,
There hills with bleating flocks adorn the scene;
Or flow'ry lawns, or shades of tufted trees,
Or waters quivering to the temper'd breeze!
Thus all combin'd the ravish'd fancy strike,
And leave it at a loss—where most to like.
 Directed hence along the carpet grass
By three fair statues to the left we pass.
Where thro' the bath[6] descending is convey'd   60
The bason,—falling from a broad cascade;
While thro' the ruin'd arch[7] the waters break,
And form below a wide extended lake;
Whose distant borders sylvan scenes unfold,
Such as the huntress-Goddess us'd of old;
When rash Actæon spy'd the heav'nly maid,
And with his forfeit life the folly paid.
 Close by the lake our progress we persued;
To the fair hermitage[8] conceal'd in wood
Whence wide beneath the blue expanse was seen,   70
Reflecting from its wave the trembling green!

---

4. A Gothic temple 70 foot high on the brow of the hill, to the right, intended to be dedicated to Liberty.
5. The north avenue to the house compos'd of tall Trees.
6. The Cold Bath receives the water from the Octagon and discharges it by a Cascade of 3 sheets of water into a large lake.
7. One of these sheets glides thro' an arch, or piece of ruine, artifically cover'd with evergreens, under which lye the statues of two river gods.
8. The Hermitage is seated in a rising wood on the banks of this lake.

Thence thro' the windings of the artful shade,
Thy temple, beauteous Venus, we survey'd;[9]
Before, fit emblem of the lover's view,
Stand the first foes[10] which nature ever knew;
Fit emblem, goddess, of thy cruel pow'r,
Which oft has bath'd the warring world in gore;
Has smil'd to set the dearest friends at strife,
And make the brother snatch the brother's life:
Yet mild at first, thy savage yoke appears,   80
And like this scene a beauteous prospect wears;
For scenes like this, thy fatal flame inspire,
Unnerve the soul—and kindle soft desire!
While amorous birds with music fill the grove,
And every breathing zephyr whispers love!
Within the dome see sportive Cupids play,
And clap their silver wings—and seem to say—
"Now let him love, who never felt the pain,
Before who lov'd—here let him love again!"[11]
    Hence thro' a wood with opening vistas grac'd,   90
(At each some rural termination plac'd)
The west pavillion to the eye succeeds,
Whence to the house the fair avenue leads;
Plac'd in the midst—and sacred to his fame,
Rises the pyramid with Vanbrugh's name.[12]
Here, wondrous architect!—repos'd receive,
The grateful honours Cobham loves to give;
Here like his gardens shall thy mem'ry bloom,

9. The Hortus Veneris is a square building designed by Mr Kent, the inside decorated with painting by Mr Slatea, here are the bustos of Nero, Vespasian, Cleopatra, and Faustina.
10. The statues of Cain and Abel.
11. The inscription on the frize from Catullus.
   Nunc amet, qui nondum amavit.
   Quique amavit, nunc amet.
12. An Egyptian pyramid 60 foot high sacred to the memory of Sir Jn Vanbrugh, with this inscription.
   Inter plurima hortorum horum ædificia a Johanne Vanbrugh, equite, designata, hanc pyramidem illius memoriæ sacram voluit esse Cobham.

Nor cou'dst thou wish a more distinguish'd tomb.
In the next dome from vulgar thought conceal'd,   100
This wise inscription stands to sight reveal'd,*
"Life is a feast—enjoy it while you may,
When age comes on—'tis time to steal away,
Least laughing youth remind thee of the rule,
Nothing so foolish as a doating fool."
⌐ Now by the wood, which rises to the right,
The opening field[13] relieves the crowded sight,
Here great Alcides, firm in marble plac'd,
Holds the expiring son of Earth embrac'd;
Just image Cobham, of thy victor toil,   110
Which tam'd the genius of the rugged soil;
Which gave the face of nature pow'r to warm,
And soften'd every blemish to a charm.
Hence to th' Augustine cave[14] our way we sped,
A moss-grown cell, with grateful umbrage spread.
Such blameless hermits held in days of old,
Ere priest-craft grew—or heav'n was priz'd for gold;
Plain is the scene—and well befits the heart
That never stain'd its innocence with art.
As the skill'd painter captivates the sight,   120
By nicely intermingling shade and light;
So in these happy scenes, each object plac'd,
Throws beauty round, and charms the finest taste:
So just the contraste—and the point so true,
Tis all that nature—all that art can do!
In sweet delusion is the fancy lost,
Nor knows attention where to settle most!

* The inscription is from Horace.
    Lusisti satis, edisti satis, atque bibisti,
    Tempus abire tibi—ne potum largius æquo
    Rideat et pulset lasciva decentius ætas.

13. The statues of Hercules and Anteus are placed at the entrance to
the field which is inclosed with a staked fence in the military way.

14. St Augustine's cave is a cell form'd of moss and roots of trees
interwoven, with a straw couch in the inside, and some inscriptions
in Monkish Latin verse. The situation is quite natural and simple.

Thus from the cave thro the receding green,
Thy temple, son of Semele was seen;[15]
Pictur'd within thy mystick rite advance,   130
And nymphs and satyrs round thy Thyrsus dance;
Such was the jovial triumph once thou led,
When India first ador'd thy mitred head!
When thy gay car submissive tygers drew,
And men the genial power of Bacchus knew:
From hence disclos'd a beauteous prospect lies,
West as the setting sun adorns the skies!
Where Aylesbury her golden vale extends,
And clos'd with purple hills the landskip ends.

But solemn scenes demand th' attentive muse,   140
Such as the Druids lov'd of old to chuse;
For lo conspicuous[16] stands the awful grove
Sacred to Woden, and the Saxon Jove:
Around the central altar seem to stand,
The gods ador'd by Hengist's[17] valiant band;
Life seems each breathing figure to inform,
A godlike freedom, and a noble scorn!
O glorious race! O nation dear to fame!
Eternal founders of the British name!
From whom exalted Albion grateful draws   150
Her long-establish'd rights—her sacred laws.
Tho in the Gulph of wasting time were lost
Each antient monument your name can boast,
Yet in this hallow'd shrine shall one remain,
While Freedom lives to bless Britannia's plain!

15. The Temple of Bacchus is of brick, the inside decorated with paintings by Mr Slatea.
16. The Saxon temple is an altar plac'd in an open grove, round which the 7 deities of this nation, that give name to the days of the week, are placed. The statues are all finished, and the scene solemn. Their names are Sunna for Sunday; Mona, or Luna, Monday; Tiw answering to Tuesday; Woden the Saxon Mars, to Wednesday; Thor or Thuner the Saxon Jove, to Thursday; Friga, the Saxon Pallas and Venus, to Friday; and Seatern, the Saxon Saturn, to Saturday.
17. Hengist was the first Saxon captain or leader who enter'd Britain. He founded the kingdom of Kent.

As darts the sun oblique his varied rays,
When thro' the fleecy cloud his lustre plays,
Here deepens to a gloom the varied green,
There beams a light—and shifts the shadowy scene;
But when the obvious vapour melts away,   160
The boundless prospect brightens into day.
So hitherto inchanted had we stray'd
Thro' light and shade, from charm to charm betray'd;
Now issuing from the covert, with surprize,
Th' unbounded landskip open'd to our eyes;[18]
Whence south, its dome the fair Rotunda rears,
Plac'd to the east Equestrian George[19] appears:
Oppos'd—new walks[20] o'erlook the forest lawn,
Where sport the peaceful deer and wanton fawn;
Full in the midst enthron'd like beauty's queen,   170
Surrounded by her graces Stowe is seen;[21]
And in the chrystal mirrour[22] plac'd below,
Beholds her every charm reflected glow!
Where snowy swans along the surface glide,
And rear their stately necks with graceful pride;
Wide from before a long succession spreads,
Of distant woods, green hills, and flow'ry meads!
O'er the free scene expatiates pleas'd the sight,
And all the soul is lost in sweet delight!

18. Nelson's seat is an airy recess to the N.W. of the house, from whence there is an open prospect.

19. In the front at the head of the canal, is the Equestrian statue of his late Majesty in armour with this inscription from Virgil.
    In medio mihi Cæsar erit;
    Et viridi in campo signum de marmore ponam
    Propter aquam.

20. Opposite to Nelson's seat N.E. is making a new bastion to answer it, with some grand walks by the side of a lawn in the park, which is well stor'd with deer.

21. The North front extends, with the offices, 640 foot in breadth, having an open view bounded by a semi-circle of trees at some miles distance.

22. Before the Front is a circular bason with swans.

Behind, disclos'd the gay Parterre is seen,   180
With vases deck'd[23] and banks of living green;
Here shelter'd all Hesperia's treasures bloom,
And the bright Orange sheds its rich perfume!
While placid as they rise on every hand,
In Cobham's smile the favour'd muses stand;
And Phœbus points to the celestial quire,
The scenes[24] that best the poet's flame inspire!
And bids them here, expell'd their native Greece,
Attune the Lyre, and sing the sweets of peace!
Conducted hence, thro' the declining shade,   190
Thy statue, great Augustus[25] rears its head;
A stately column's fair Corinthian height,
Bears with triumphant air the royal weight;
Which seems a smile majestic to bestow,
As pleas'd that Britain can produce a Stowe!
Now thro' the deep'ning wood's projected gloom,
To Dido's cave with devious step we come!
Where the dim twilight of the arch above,
Seems to express the queen's disastrous love!
For semblant such of old[26] the fatal bow'r,   200
Where Venus led her in ill-omen'd hour,
When first her heart the sweet delusion found,
As yet unconscious of a future wound!
Next to the fair ascent our steps we trac'd
Whence shines afar the bold Rotunda plac'd;
The artful dome Ionic columns bear

---

23. Behind the S. front lyes the parterre with the statues of Apollo
and the nine Muses and two orangeries. But it is thought this
will be altered to make room for a nobler prospect.
24. *Scriptorum omne chorus amat nemus et fugit urbes.* Hor.
25. The statue of his present Majesty is erected on a Corinthian
pillar, with this inscription.
    Georgio Augusto.
26. Dido's cave is an antique dark stone building with this
inscription from Virgil.
    Speluncam Dido, Dux et Trojanus eandem
    Deveniunt.

Light as the fabric swells in ambient air,
Beneath unshrin'd the Tuscan Venus[27] stands,
And beauty's queen the beauteous scene commands:
The fond beholder sees with sweet surprize,   210
Streams glitter, lawns appear, and forests rise—
Here thro' thick shades alternate buildings break
There thro' its borders steals the silver lake;
A soft variety delights the soul,
And harmony resulting crowns the whole!
　　Now by the long canal we gently turn,
Whose verdant sides romantic scenes adorn;
As objects thro' the broken ground we see,
And there a statue rises, there a tree!
Here in an amphitheatre of green,   220
With slopes set off which form a rural scene,
On four Ionick pillars rais'd to sight,
Beams Carolina[28] Britain's late delight!
Here the bright queen her heav'nly form displays,
Eternal subject of the Muse's praise;
But faint all praise her merit to impart,
Whose mem'ry lives in every British heart!
　　Now leave we, devious, the declining plain,
A while to wander thro' the woodland scene;
Here where six centring walks united meet,   230
Morpheus[29] invites us to his still retreat;
And while the tide of life uncertain flows,
"Bids you indulge your self, and taste repose!"

27. The Rotunda is rais'd on Ionic pillars on a gentle rise, beneath it
    the Medicean Venus gilt, on a pedestal of blue marble. The
    building is the design of Sir Jn Vanbrugh. The views from hence
    are inchanting.
28. The late queen's statue is erected on 4 ionic columns, in a green
    amphitheatre laid out in the rural way, on the pedestal is this
    inscription,
    Honori, laudi, virtuti, divæ Carolinæ.
29. The sleeping parlour is plac'd in a close wood where six walks
    meet. It is a square building with these words on the frize.
    Cum omnia sint in incerto, fave tibi.

But stop my muse—I feel a conscious fear,
As if conceal'd divinity was near!
What do I see?—what solemn views arise!
What wonders open to my thoughtful eyes!
Midst purling streams in awful beauty drest,
The shrine of Ancient Virtue[30] stands confess'd;
A Doric pile! by studious Cobham plac'd,   240
To shew the world the worth of ages past;
When innocence—when truth still found regard,
And cherish'd merit had its due reward!

  Within four graceful statues honour'd stand,
Inspire attention, and esteem command;
"Epaminondas[31] first in arms renown'd,
Whose glorious aim his country's freedom crown'd
Born in each social virtue to excell,
With whom the Theban glory rose—and fell!"
"Lycurgus[32] next, in steddy virtue great,   250
Who for duration form'd the Spartan state;
And wealth expelling, with her baneful train,
Left a republick worth the name of men!"
"There Socrates, th' Athenian[33] wise and good,
With more than mortal sanctity endued;
Who freed philosophy from useless art,
And show'd true science was to mend the heart."

30. The temple of Ancient Virtue is a Rotunda of the Doric order by
    Mr Kent.
31.   I. Epaminondas.
    Cujus virtute, prudentia, verecundia, Thebanorum respublica
    libertatem; simul & imperium, Disciplinam bellicam, civilem, &
    domesticam accepit, eoque amisso, perdidit.
32.   II. Lycurgus.
    Qui summo cum consilio, inventis legibus, omnemque contra corruptelam
    munitis optime, Pater Patriæ, libertatem firmissimam, & mores sanctissimos,
    expulsa cum divitiis, avaritia, luxuria, libidine, in multa secula, civibus
    suis instituit.
33.   III. Socrates.
    Qui corruptissima in civitate innocens, bonorum hortator, unici cultor dei,
    ab inutili otio, & vanis disputationibus, ad officia vitæ & societatis
    commoda, philosophiam avocavit, hominum sapientissimus.

"Last stands the prince of bards, whose deathless lay
Does virtue in exalted verse convey;[34]
Sets every passion in its native light,   260
And fills the soul with terror and delight!"
"These[35] point, the way to reach immortal praise,
Is life on publick Virtue's base to raise!
And shew that goodness and our country's love
Exalt us to the blissful seats above;
Where bards repose, and godlike patriots smile,
And glorious heroes rest from earthly toil!
While, like the ruin plac'd in view beneath,
The tyrant and oppressor rot in death;
All born of vice devoted to decay,[36]   270
And hastening like the gliding brook away!"
     Now leaving with regret the solemn wood,
We by the winding stream our course persued;
Where stands the lonesome grotto[37] sweetly plac'd,
With all the art of sportive nature grac'd:
Two neighb'ring domes[38] on spiral columns rise,
With shells and min'rals spangled to the eyes.
Whence, still directed by the winding stream,
Amus'd, we to the three-arch'd building came.
Hence west the church adorns the opening height,   280

34.   IV. Homerus.
   Qui poetarum princeps idem & maximus, virtutis præco, & immortalitatis largitor, divino carmine, ad pulchre audendum, & patiendum fortiter, omnibus gentibus notus, omnes incitat.

35. Inscription over the one door,
   Justitiam cole & pietatem, quæ cum sit magna in parentibus & propinquis, tum in patria maxima est. Ea vita est via in cælum & in hunc cætum eorum qui jam vixerunt.

36. Over the other,
   Charum esse civem, bene de republica mereri, laudari, diligi, coli, gloriosum est: metui vero & in odio esse, invidiosum, detestabile, imbecillum, caducum.

37. This grotto is to be properly decorated.

38. Near this on the opposite banks of the river are two pavillions, the domes supported by spiral columns; the one ornamented with shells as the other is to be with pebbles.

Eastward the spacious pond relieves the sight:
In which of form Chinese a structure[39] lies,
Where all her wild grotesques display'd surprise;
Within Japan her glittering treasure yields,
And ships of amber sail on golden fields!
In radiant clouds are silver turrets found,
And mimic glories glitter all around.
    Soon tired of these, the river next we cross'd,
To scenes[40] where fancy is in wonder lost;
Such were th' Elysian fields described of old,   290
By raptur'd bards who blest the age of gold;
Such gay romantic prospects rise around,
With such profusion smiles the flow'ry ground!
So steals th' ambrosial pleasure on the mind,
We think 'tis heav'n—and leave the world behind.
So shine with native pomp the realms of light,
So pure the æther, and the scenes so bright!
Hail sacred spot—may no unhallowed tread!
Profane thy beauties, or thy sweets invade;
Hence all ye slaves of vice and pow'r, away: 300
Here none approach, —but who are fit to stay!
    See where the guardian of these blissful seats,
Discerning Hermes on the assembly waits![41]
And ranks, to fame each British worthy known,
Who here distinguish'd, finds a just renown!

39. The Chinese house is situated in a pond, and you enter it by a bridge adorn'd with Chinese vases with flow'rs in them. It is a square building with 4 Lettices, and covered with sail cloth to preserve the lustre of the paintings; in it is a Chinese lady as if asleep, her hands covered by her gown. In the pond are the figures of two Chinese birds about the size of a duck, which move with the wind as if living. The outside of the house is painted in the taste of that nation by Mr Slatea; the inside is India japann'd work.

40. Hence you cross the shell bridge to the Elysian fields, which well deserve that name.

41. In the niche of a pyramid is placed Mercury with this inscription.

Campos ducit ad Elysios.

"Those happy Kings who flattery's voice disdain'd,*
Who in their subjects hearts with glory reign'd;
Patriots, who for their country joy'd to bleed;
Or Statesmen who the publick weal decreed;
Poets who scorn'd the muses to profane,   310
Nor courted vice, nor wrote for sordid gain:
Or those by arts of use to human kind,
Who toil'd to leave a worthy name behind.
Names that for virtue's godlike ends were born,
To bless, to save, to counsel, or adorn."
Serene in justice and in goodness great,
Here[42] Alfred shines the founder of the state!
Here Edward smiles, as when the world's delight,
In peace belov'd, and dreadful in the fight!
Here stands Eliza, empress of the main,   320
Who Europe free'd—and humbled haughty Spain!
William whose sword his native land reliev'd,
And Britain from impending fate retriev'd!
Here Raleigh lives, the man who greatly fell,
For speaking truly—and for acting well!
And Drake who first with naval glory crown'd,
Bore Britain's fame the spacious globe around!
With Hampden firm assertor of her laws,
And proto-martyr in the glorious cause!
      There[43] Gresham does his true encomium claim,   330
And points the Merchants honourable name:
There Jones, great Architect! who taught our Isle
With Greek and Roman elegance to smile:

---

*   Below on a square marble are these lines of Virgil.
        Hic manus ob patriam pugnando vulnera passi,
        Quique pii vates, et Phœbo digna locuti,
        Inventas aut qui vitam excoluere per artes,
        Quique sui memores alios fecere merendo.

42. On the right are the busts of K. Alfred, Edward the black prince,
    Q. Elizabeth, K. William III, Sir Walter Raleigh, Sir Francis Drake
    and Mr Hampden, with proper inscriptions.

43. To the left those of Sir Thomas Gresham, Inigo Jones, Milton,
    Shakespear, Newton, Locke, and Ld Bacon.

Milton, whose genius, like his subject high,
Gave him beyond material bounds to fly!
And manly Shakespear, whose extensive mind
Could fathom all the passions of mankind!
There Newton lives, whose sight was form'd to trace
Deep nature's laws, and clear her mystick face!
And Bacon, first who left the jangling schools   340
To fix philosophy on certain rules.
With Locke, who, shewing truth in reasons light,
Taught the instructed mind to judge aright.
    Two living worthies[44] here distinguish'd breathe,
And taste of spotless fame[45] before their death;
By no inscription is their merit shown,
Their names suffice to eternize the stone!
For Barnard's virtue scorns all borrow'd rays,
And Pope's exalted merit[46] baffles praise!
    Now passing onward from th' Elysian ground,   350
An enigmatic Monument we found;
Sacred to honest Fido's blameless name,
A foreigner of no ignoble fame:
Much art is shown his virtues to commend;
"A tender husband—and a faithful friend;
No Bigot—nature was his constant rule,
And tho' conversant with the great—no fool.
Think this not flatt'ry, tho' so much in vogue,
'Tis real truth—for Fido—was a dog."[47]
    To freedom's shrine, across the level field,   360
Still circling to the right[48] our course we held;
Plac'd on the summit's lofty brow it stands,
And all the wide extended view commands.
Descending hence new objects meet the eyes;

44. Also those of Sir John Barnard and Mr Pope but without
    inscriptions.
45. *Vita priore frui.*
46. *Cui male si palpere recalcitret undique tutus.*
47. The monument of signior Fido, an Italian dog.
48. Temple of liberty. (See line 44)

Spread to the left a long plantation lies;[49]
While from the right two winding Rivers bend,
And to the opening Basin smooth descend.
Here the Palladian bridge[50] observed before
At distance, pleas'd we nearer now explore.
Where are choice busts antique and modern, seen   370
"And the glad world pays homage to its queen."
    Now to th' imperial cabinet[51] we come,
Of cubic form the bright historic room!
Where Monarchs wholesome counsel may receive,
Since Cæsars the instructive Lesson give;
There Titus' motto tells he mourn'd the day
In which his goodness shed no friendly ray!
The delegated sword of Trajan shows,
Himself not spar'd, if rank'd with virtue's foes:
There mild Aurelius, friend of human kind,   380
Conveys this maxim from his generous mind,
"If rais'd to regal pow'r, such mandates give,
As, chang'd, you would a private man receive."
Lessons like these humanity impart,
And bend to mercy ev'n the tyrant's heart.
    Now thro' a stately gate we take our way,
And the surprizing terras pleas'd survey;
Stretch'd to the eye the lineal walk extends,
And bounded by the shrine of Venus ends;[52]
Here Friendship's temple strikes the ravish'd sight, 390
With finish'd symmetry, and graceful height;
Manly as is the theme it means to grace,

49. The walk of abeal trees.
50. The Palladian bridge, where is a collection of bustoes, also the
    figure of Britannia receiving homage from the four quarters of
    the world, painted by Mr Slatea.
51. The imperial closet is a room of a cubic form with 3 sides, on
    one, the figure of Titus Cæsar with this motto *Diem perdidi*; on
    the second, Trajan with this inscription, *Pro me, si merear, in me*;
    on the third Marcus Aurelius, with this sentence, *Ita reges
    imperator, ut si privatus regi velis.*
52. This noble terrass is near 3000 foot long.

The lofty square displays its Doric face;[53]
For Cobham this devoted frame intends[54]
For Virtue's fav'rites and for Britain's friends!
 Not far from hence dear Congreve's urn is shown,
His worth recorded on the lasting stone;[55]
Nor greater honour could the Roman boast,
When godlike Scipio wept his Terence lost!
 Now by the octagon our course we hold,   400
Where laughing satyrs beauty's queen behold;
While the gay goddess[56] careless of their smile,
Spreads every charm, industrious to beguile!
And now the sweet delightful circuit done,
Our progress ended—where it first begun.
 Thus has the Muse with feeble wing essay'd
To paint the wonders of th' inchanted shade;
And, fond the charms of nature to explore,
Rov'd, like the studious bee, from flow'r to flow'r;
Stopp'd by each pleasing object she could meet,   410
To sip some fragrance, or collect some sweet.
But as where Britain's Fair assembled shine,
The rays of beauty spread a light divine;
So here, where nature does her triumphs show,
And with majestick hand adorns a Stowe;
Description fails—all fancy is too mean,
They only can conceive it—who have seen!

53. The temple of Friendship a noble structure of the Doric order. In the cieling is Britannia with some other figures; one holds a Label with these words, *The reign of K. Edward III*; another, a scroll with *The reign of Q. Elizabeth*; a third, with *The reign of* ——— the rest being covered with her mantle.

54. In this are the following 10 bustos of my Lord and his illustrious friends—viz. The P. of Wales, Earls of Westmoreland, Chesterfield, and Marchmont, Lords Cobham, Gower and Bathurst, Richard Grenville, Will. Pit, and George Lyttelton Esqrs.

55. Mr Congreve's monument with this inscription. *Ingenio acri, faceto, expolito, Moribusque urbanis, candidis, facillimis, Gulielmi Congreve, hoc qualecunque desiderii sui solamen simul et monumentum posuit Cobham. 1736.*

56. A dancing Venus with three satyrs on the right side of the octagon.

To the author of the poem on Lord C–B–M's Gardens

Boyse's poem provoked this reply, which was printed the following year (1743) in the March number of the *Gentleman's Magazine*. The unknown author asked why so much had been spent on pagan temples while the parish church was neglected. The poem may reflect the common contemporary belief that Lord Cobham was an atheist, though, like many Englishmen of his generation, he would probably have been described more accurately as a Deist.

```
        While art and nature, taste and fancy joyn,
        To form and finish C–b–m's grand design;
        The prospect wide, extended wider still,
        Spread by thy magic lay o'er Britain's isle;
        While all admire, and all to praise contend;
        Blame would against the publick voice offend.
        Yet, as nought human can perfection claim,
        I, tho' no connoisseur, presume to blame
        One fault in beauteous Stowe; Stowe's poet too
        Seems conscious censure's just, or he's untrue.          10
            While stately temples numberless arise,
        Temples devote to heathen deities:
        On which is spar'd no cost, no grace, no art,
        (Such their importance) genius could impart;
        And thy sweet numbers unrestrained flow,
        Their pomp and proud magnificence to show;
        One single line is all thou canst afford
        To decorate the temple of the lord.
        Shall greater honour be to Bacchus given,
        And strumpet Venus than the God of heav'n?              20
        Are banish'd Thor and Woden then restor'd?
        And more than Christ, our present God, ador'd?
        In christian land, gods Pagan to prefer!
        Christian! is this in taste or character?
        Our country God eclips'd by foreign! hence
        To boasted patriot virtue vain pretence.
            Oh C–b–m! deign God's house to beautifie,
        Nor let this only place neglected lye.
        Where decency and order so much shine,
        Sure decency is due to things divine.                   30
        Let this be paid—Morpheus's motto* raze,
        And Stowe will be allow'd to want no Grace.
        *Cum omnia sunt in incerto, fave tibi.
```

Anonymous (1742)

The extraordinary thing about this visitor is that he toured the showplaces of England for a month, analysing carefully what he saw and illustrating his journal with plans of buildings and garden lay-outs, and yet he never mentioned a single architect or designer by name, not even at Greenwich nor Blenheim. He began and finished his journey at Norwich, and he was familiar enough with Cambridge to use it as a standard by which to judge, none too favourably, the lay-out of several Oxford colleges. His identity is unknown, but it seems possible that he was a practising surveyor, collecting ideas for potential clients in East Anglia in the course of his touring holiday.

He was years ahead of his time in seeing the need for plans of the lay-out and the garden buildings, and though his pen and wash sketch-plans are crude, they are essential to his description, and so they have been reproduced and inserted in their context.

A Plan of Lord Cobhams Garden.

from *Some Observations made in a Journey begun June the 7th, and finish'd July the 9th 1742*

The Plan of two Dorick Temples
which are adorn'd with a Pedament.

The water in the Octagon is 8 or 9 Foot Deep above the Lake leading to Venus. It falls in 3 Sheets down severall Steps, upon which are scattered Pebbles and Stones diverting and retarding the Current and entertaining both the Eyes and Ears; the Slope all about is planted with Shrubs, Greens and Flowers and among them are plac'd Statutes of Satyrs, a Venus, etc. Over the midle Cascade, is an open Arch representing a piece of Ruin and on

[KEY TO THE PLAN ON THE OPPOSITE PAGE]

AA, represents 2 Dorick Temples	SS, two Shell Temples
B, an Obelisk standing in an Octagon Bason	T, A 3 Arch'd Building
	U, an India House
C, a Cascade	W, the Temple of Worthy's
D, the Temple of Venus	X, a Bridge
E, Gibbs's Temple rais'd on an Eminence	Y, a Roman Closet
F, first Roman Temple	Z, the Temple of Friendship
G, A Pyramid	1, A Pebble House
H, the Temple of Bachus	2, Congreves Monument
I, Small Obelisk	3, the end of the River
K, A Saxon Temple	4444, Grand Walks
L, the 2d Roman Temple	5, A Cascade
M, A house	66, An Avenue
N, the Rotunda	7,7, Walks
O, a Statute of his Present Majesty, on a Corinth: Column	8, A Wood House
	9, Dido's Cave
P, A Statute of Queen Caroline on 4 Ionick Columns on a Pedestal	10, the Sleeping Parlour
	11, A Witch House
Q, the Temple of Virtue	12, A Gothick Temple
R, the Hermitage	13, the Cold Bath

each side the Arch a Nich in some measure shaded with Shrubs; here repose a Couple of River Gods on their Urns and out of them seem to Pour the Water down the Steps.

Between A, D, and C, 3, is a Grove with a little winding shady Walk, yielding a Retreat from the great Walk above, and that on the Banks of the Lake.

Between 4, F and E, G, is another Grove of Serpentine Walks presenting you now and then a little Area, decorated with Statues.

E, N, C, 3, is almost wholly taken up with Meadow and Pasture Ground, as is the Space between 5, 4 and X, and the meeting of the Rivers on the other side of the Garden.

F the 1st Roman Temple rises square one Story upon which is plac'd a Piramid, in it are 4, fine Roman Statues. The other F without the Garden, is built in the same manner and inhabited, between 'em is a passage to the House up an Avenue.

L the Second Roman Temple is of this Shape.

Its in the Ionick, the Pillars support the Entrance and over the order is an Attick, on each side are Piers riseing up higher than the Order.

From the 1st Roman Temple to the 2d, the great Walk presents you with an Extended Prospect. If you leave it, and turn to the Egyptian Pyramid, you are buried in Woods and lead by meandring Walks to the House built with Roots; to Bachus's Temple, having a little Area before it, grac'd with Statues and an Obelisk, and from hence into a Circular Area having an Alter in its Center and the Statues of the Saxon Gods at equall distance in the Circumference.

The North and South Fronts of the House consists of 2 Storys, 13 Windows each, the North has an Hexstyle Ionick

Portico and Pedamt, the South hath 2 Orders, an hextile Portico in the Dorick, and an hextile Pedament in the Ionick.

N, the Rotunda hath a Dome suported by 10 Ionick Pillars, in the midle is a Statue of a Medicean Venus rais'd on a Round Pedestal.

Q, The Temple of Virtue is of the following Shape, the Pillars are Ionick, forming a Portico round the Dome springing from the Wall.

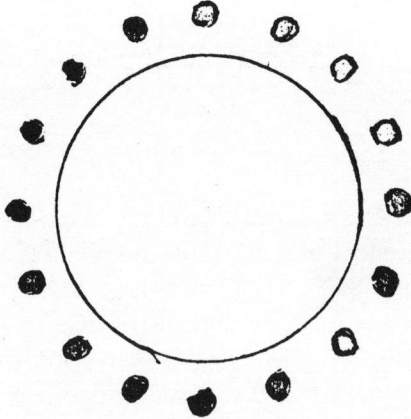

Before the South Front is a Semicircular Area it has its Bottom adorn'd with the Statues of Apollo and the Muses equally disposed on each side of the Avenue.

R, is situated at the Head of the River. In it is a Statue of Venus, retired from bathing, and a considerable Quantity of sparkling Rock Stones, with which it is design'd to be enrich'd, the building within is of this Frame.

And it's Front resembles Richmonds Hermitage.

S, has a shell'd Dome resting on 6, wreathed Pillars, cover'd with the same materials.

From hence winding with the River, you pass by T (an agreeable Recess on the Banks of it) to U, a square building in a Pond, adorn'd in the Chinese manner. From hence you are led into the Elysian Fields, a delightfull and ravishing Grove on the side of the River, and pass by W, situated in a spot a little more open than the rest, it is a single Wall this Shape.

West.

It's Niches are fill'd with the Busts of Pope, Gresham, Jones, Milton, Shakespear, Lock, Newton and Bacon on the Left; and K. Alfred, Edward Prince of Wales, Eliz, Wm. the 3rd, Raleigh, Drake, Hambden and Barnard on the Right; the Middle part rises square as high as the Sides are carryed, over it is plac'd a pyramid, having a Nych; the River above 5 is three or 4 feet higher than below, the Water pasing under the ground, issues between the Stones with which the Cascade is faced and trickles gently down 'em.

X, Has 5, Arches, the largest in the Middle; the 2, Next in size are the outer one's, upon the Bridge is an Order of Ionick Pillars, standing on Pedestals, which form the Ballustrade to the Bridge, the 6, Pillars over the 3 Midle Arches, support nothing above the Entablature; over the others are circular Pedaments and between 'em Arches, the Passage on to the

A Plan of the upper Part of the Bridge.

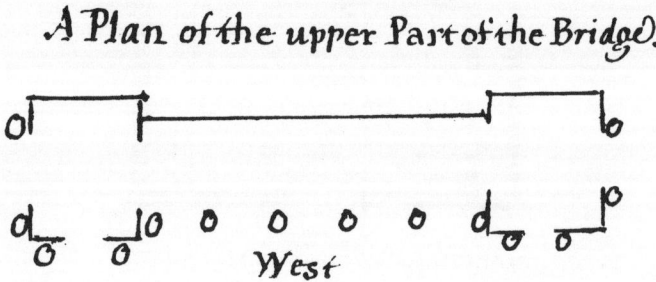

West

Bridge is adornd in the same manner. The side opposite to the 6, Colums is enrichd with a Basso Relivo and that opposite to the Arches with a painting.

Y, Is a small Square Room.

Z, Is a large square Room having 3 of its sides adorn'd with Dorick Pillars or Pillasters.

Between Z, A and BX is a Grove resembling that 1st mentioned; in it before the River is a Peble Recess of which A is the Plan and B the Elevation.

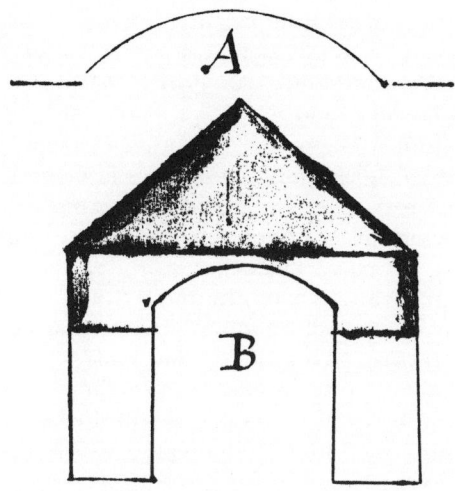

From whence walking along the Banks and Passing by Congreve's Monument you are led to the Octagon Bason, and bid to take leave of the Garden.

The neighbouring Park is compos'd of Wood and Avenues, it yeilds such a plenty of the one and such a variety of the others, as render it highly entertaining; the Visto's open every Way upon the Hills and display by degrees the whole Country to you.

(BL Add. MS 22926, ff. 65-71)

James Thomson *(1700 – 1748)*

Born and educated in Scotland, James Thomson travelled south in 1725, and made his living for some years as a private tutor. He gained fame as a writer with *The Seasons*, a long poem in four parts, of which the collected edition came out in 1730; and his *Britannia*, attacking Walpole's policy of peace at any price, brought him to the notice of the politicians.

His first contact with Stowe may have been through Bubb Doddington, a cousin of Lord Cobham, whom he met soon after his arrival in England. But when Cobham fell out with Walpole and George II in the mid-1730s and Stowe became a centre of the 'Patriot' Opposition, Thomson was taken on as propagandist for the cause. His poem *Liberty* (1735-6) was dedicated to Frederick, Prince of Wales, the figurehead of the Opposition Patriots, and this was followed by a number of other political compositions. All are now forgotten—except "Rule, Britannia" from *The Masque of Alfred*—and Thomson's fame rests secure on that and *The Seasons*. A revised and enlarged version of this was published in 1744, and it is from an additional passage in the third part, *Autumn*, that the following excerpt is taken.

A couple of generations later, in about 1800, the 1st Marquess of Buckingham put up a small building of white marble beside a path a short distance upstream from the Elysian Fields. It was arranged that water from a nearby spring should be brought to it and fall into two marble bowls, one below the other, as it still does today. This is called the Seasons Fountain, which is dedicated to the memory of James Thomson, to record his happy association with Stowe.

The text follows J.L. Robertson's Oxford edition of 1908, with the addition of some capital letters from the 1788 collected edition of Thomson's works.

from *Autumn (1744)*

Or is this gloom too much? Then lead, ye Powers
That o'er the garden and the rural seat
Preside, which, shining through the cheerful land
In countless numbers, blest Britannia sees—   1040
Oh! lead me to the wide extended walks,
The fair majestic paradise of Stowe!
Not Persian Cyrus on Ionia's shore
E'er saw such sylvan scenes, such various art
By genius fired, such ardent genius tamed
By cool judicious art, that in the strife
All-beauteous Nature fears to be outdone.
And there, O Pitt! thy country's early boast,
There let me sit beneath the sheltered slopes,
Or in that Temple where, in future times,   1050
Thou well shalt merit a distinguished name,
And, with thy converse blest, catch the last smiles
Of Autumn beaming o'er the yellow woods.
While there with thee the enchanted round I walk,
The regulated wild, gay fancy then
Will tread in thought the groves of Attic Land;
Will from thy standard taste refine her own,
Correct her pencil to the purest truth
Of Nature, or, the unimpassioned shades
Forsaking, raise it to the human mind.   1060
Oh, if hereafter she with juster hand
Shall draw the tragic scene, instruct her thou
To mark the varied movements of the heart,
What every decent character requires,
And every passion speaks! Oh, through her strain
Breathe thy pathetic eloquence, that moulds
The attentive senate, charms, persuades, exalts,
Of honest zeal the indignant lightning throws,
And shakes Corruption on her venal throne!
While thus we talk, and through Elysian Vales   1070
Delighted rove, perhaps a sigh escapes—

What pity, Cobham! thou thy verdant files
Of ordered trees shouldst here inglorious range,
Instead of squadrons flaming o'er the field,
And long-embattled hosts! when the proud foe,
The faithless vain disturber of mankind,
Insulting Gaul, has roused the world to war;
When keen, once more, within their bounds to press
Those polished robbers, those ambitious slaves,
The British Youth would hail thy wise command,   1080
Thy tempered ardour and thy veteran skill.

Page 49

Grecian Temple

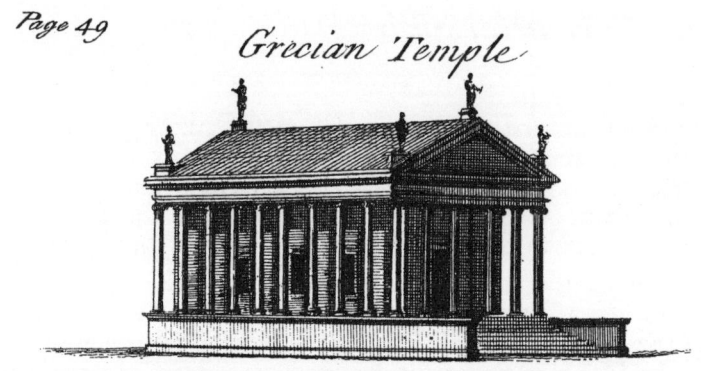

Bickham

Capt: Grenville's Monument

Acc.? to Act 174

Engraving by George Bickham
from *The Beauties of Stow*

Benton Seeley (1716 – 1795)

By publishing the first comprehensive guidebook to a country seat, Benton Seeley has earned his place in garden history. Such publications were already known in Italy and nowadays we take them for granted, but during the 1740s they were a genre almost unknown in England. An isolated example had appeared nearly twenty years earlier, in 1726, for the house and garden of Josiah Diston at Epsom, and guides had been brought out for visitors to Wilton (1731) and Houghton (1743), but both of these were essentially catalogues of pictures for connoisseurs. So when Seeley, writing-master in Buckingham, the country town three miles from Stowe, produced *A Description of the Gardens of Lord Viscount Cobham at Stow* in 1744, he was pioneering a novel kind of publication.

His starting point was the description of Stowe contained in the appendix to Defoe's *Tour* (1742). This had to be adapted and re-arranged into a sequence which followed a visitor's normal circuit of the gardens. It was intentionally an objective catalogue, "a plain Account", as Seeley wrote in his short preface, "a simple, regular Relation of every Thing in Order". Enquiries, he continued, had often been made for a description of this kind, and he presented it to the public "to save the Trouble of taking down the Inscriptions or the Names of the Buildings".

This modest venture met, in Seeley's own words, with "great, and indeed unexpected, Success", which must have included the approval of Stowe's noble owner, for in the following year (1745) an extended edition of thirty-four pages appeared, with a fulsome dedication to Lord Cobham. Further editions were required in each of the years up to 1749, all of them "corrected and enlarg'd" to keep pace with the continuous expansion of the gardens.

Things were clearly going well for Seeley, who changed the description of himself from "writing-master" to "bookseller and stationer", dropping George Norris, the "peruke-maker", from the partnership, and arranging for his guidebook to be available in London, at Rivington's in St. Paul's Churchyard. There were problems ahead, when another publisher tried to break into the Stowe tourist market; but after this threat had been dealt with, Seeley and his family were to continue publishing the guidebooks for the next seventy years. It was not long before their expanding business enabled them to establish their own printing press in Buckingham and set up as publishers in London, where their firm continued publishing until 1978. In other fields as well the Seeley family was to make its name, producing several authors and scholars in the nineteenth century, of whom the historian Sir John Seeley was the most distinguished.

A
DESCRIPTION
OF THE
GARDENS
OF
Lord Viscount Cobham,
AT
STOW in Buckinghamshire.

Here Order in Variety you see,
Where all Things differ,---- yet where all agree !
A..POPE.

NORTHAMPTON:
Printed by W. Dicey ; and sold by *B. Seeley*, Writing-Master,
in *Buckingham*, and *George Norris*, Peruke-Maker, in *Newport-Pagnell*, *Bucks*. M.DCC.XLIV.

A Description of the Gardens of the Lord Viscount Cobham at Stow (1744)

PREFACE

The following Design is nothing more than to give a plain Account of the GARDENS *of the Lord* COBHAM *at* STOW: *As they are esteemed, by Persons of the most exact Taste, to be the finest in this Kingdom, and perhaps in* Europe, *such an Account cannot be altogether disagreeable or useless.*

Those who have but seldom seen them, and seen them (as every Person must have done) with Pleasure, may, by this little Assistant, have every pleasing Scene presented to their Imagination in the truest Colours; they may have their Memories refreshed at a Distance, they may have each Building and each Prospect called to their View almost as well as if they were upon the delightful Spot. The Author has taken all imaginable Care to give a simple, regular Relation of every Thing in Order as it lies disposed in the Gardens: There is not need of Art or Embellishment, they want not such mean Artifices to set them off; the exactest Description must be the greatest Encomium upon them.

Such a Description as this has often been enquired for; if such an one will be either useful or amusing, the Author gains his Point; and therefore presents it to the Publick with this View only, that it will save the Trouble of taking down the Inscriptions, or the Names of the Buildings, and be an Help to the Memories of those Numbers who have the Curiosity to see these Gardens.

A
DESCRIPTION
OF THE
GARDENS
OF
Lord Viscount *Cobham.*

At the South Entrance of the Gardens are two Pavilions supported by Doric Columns. From thence you descend to a large Octagon Piece of Water, with an Obelisk in the Center 70 Feet high, designed for a *Jet d'eau.*

An Artificial Piece of Ruin
cover'd with Ever-greens, under which lie the Statues of two River Gods; a beautiful Cascade of three Sheets of Water falls from the Octagon into a large Lake of 10 Acres.

[p.2] The Cold Bath
receives the Water from the Octagon.

The Hermitage
is seated in a rising Wood, on the Banks of the Lake.

The Statues of *Cain* and *Abel.*

The Temple dedicated to *Venus,*
with this Inscription,

Veneri Hortensi.

It is a square Building, design'd by Mr. *Kent*; the Inside adorn'd with Paintings by Mr. *Slater,* the History of which is taken from *Spencer's Fairy Queen.* Without are the Bustos of

Nero, Vespasian, Cleopatra, and *Faustina*; and on the Frize is the following Motto, alluding to the Painting in the Cave:

Nunc amet, qui nondum amavit;
Quique amavit, nunc amet.

[p.3] *Which is thus translated:*

Let him love now, who never lov'd before:
Let him who always lov'd, now love the more.

The Belvidere,
or *Gibbs*'s Building; under which is the Ice-House.

Two Pavilions
at the Entrance of the Park, with Roman Statues in one, and the other inhabited.

An Egyptian Pyramid
60 Feet high, sacred to the Memory of Sir *John Vanbrugh.* On the Outside is this Inscription:

Inter plurima hortorum horum ædificia a Johanne Vanbrugh, equite, designata, hanc pyramidem illius memoriæ sacr[am] voluit Cobham.

[p.4] *In English thus:*
Among a very great Number of Structures in these Gardens, design'd by Sir *John Vanbrugh,* Knight, *Cobham* thought fit that this Pyramid should be sacred to his Memory.

And in the Inside is:

Lusisti satis, edisti satis, atque bibisti:
Tempus abire tibi est; ne potum largius æquo
Rideat et pulset lasciva decentius ætas.

Which may be thus translated:

Enough you've sported, quaff'd the Bowl, and eat;
'Tis time that from the Banquet you retreat,
Lest Youth, more fitly frolicksome, may join
To push you, reeling, under Loads of Wine.

The Statues of *Hercules* and *Anteus*

are placed at the Entrance to the Field, which is inclosed with
a staked Fence in the Military Way.

[p.5] St. *Augustine's* Cave

is a Cell form'd of Moss and Roots of Trees interwoven, with a
Straw Couch in the Inside, and the three following Inscriptions
in Monkish Latin Verse. —The Situation is quite natural and
simple.

On the Right Hand:

> Sanctus pater Augustinus
> (Prout aliquis divinus
> Narrat) contra sensualem
> Actum Veneris lethalem
> (Audiat clericus) ex nive
> Similem puellam vivæ
> Arte mira conformabat
> Qua cum bonus vir cubabat
> Quod si fas est in errorem
> Tantum cadere doctorem
> Quæri potest, an carnalis
> Mulier potius quam nivalis
> Non sit apta ad domandum
> Subigendum debellandum
> Carnis tumidum furorem
> Et importunum ardorem
> Nam ignis igni pellitur
> Vetus ut verbum loquitur
> [p.6] Sed innuptus, hac in lite
> Appellabo te marite.

On the Left:

Apparuit mihi, nuper in Somnio cum nudis et anhelantibus
mulier Papillis & hianti suaviter [Vu]ltu—ehu! benedicite!

Cur gaudes Satana muliebrem sumere formam
Non facies Voti casti me rump[ere] normam

Heus fugite in Cellam! pulchram vitate Puellam
Nam Radix Mortis fuit olim Fœmina in Hortis

Vis fieri fortis? Noli concumbere Scortis?

In Sanctum Originem Eunuchum,
Filius Ecclesiæ Origines fortasse probetur;
Esse Patrem nunquam se sine Teste probet
Virtus diaboli est in Lumbis.

Fronting the Door:

Mente pie elatâ peragro dum dulcia Prata
   Dormiit absq: dolo pulchra Puella solo;
Multa ostendebat dum semisupina jacebat,
   Pulchrum Os divinum pectus, aperta Sinum.
[p.7] Ut vidi Mammas, concepi ex tempore Flammas,
   Et dicturus ave, dico, Maria, cave
Nam magno totus violenter turbine motus
   Pœne illam invado, poene et in ora cado.
Illa sed haud lenté surgit curritq. repenté,
   Currit et, invito me, fugit illa citó,
Fugit Causa Mali tamen Effectus Satanali
   Internoq' Meum lor vorat Igne reum;
O, Inferne Can[is] curquotidie est tibi Panis,
   Per Visus miros sollicitare Viros?
Cur Manachos velles fieri tam Carne rebelles
   Nec castæ Legi turbida Membra regi
In tibi jam Bellum dico jam triste Flagellum
   Esuriemq. paro quêis subigenda Caro

Quin abscindatur ne Pars sincera trahatur
Radix quâ solus nascitur usq. Dolus.

The Reader is desired to excuse the Translation of the foregoing
Inscription, for some particular Reasons.

The Temple of *Bacchus*

is of Brick, the Inside adorn'd with Paintings by Mr. *Slater.*

A small Obelisk, with this Inscription:

To the Memory of Robin Coucher.

[p.8] The *Saxon* Temple,

with an Altar placed in an open Grove, round which the
seven Deities of this Nation, that give Name to the Days of the
Week, were placed, which are since removed to the Gothic
Building.

Nelson's Seat

is an airy Recess to the North-West of the House, from
whence there is an open Prospect, and in it are the following
Inscriptions, describing the Painting.

On the Right Hand:

Ultra Euphratem et Tigrim
usq ad Oceanum propagata ditione
Orbis Terrarum Imperium Romæ adsignat optimus Princeps
cui super advolat Victoria
Laurigerum sertum hinc inde
utraq manu extendens
comitantibus Pietate et Abundantia in ara Constantine

[p.9] *Thus translated:*

The most excellent Prince
having extended his Power beyond the *Euphrates* and *Tygris,*

as far as the Ocean,
assigns the Empire of the World to *Rome*;
over whom flies *Victory*,
stretching forth a Laurel Crown
on each Side with both Hands,
accompany'd with *Piety* and *Plenty*, on the Altar of *Constantine*.

On the Left:

Post Obitum L. Veri
in imperio cum Marco consortis,
Roma
integram orbis Terrarum
potestatem ei et in eo contulit in Capitolio

In English thus:

After the Death of *Lucius Verus*,
Partner in the Empire with *Marcus*,
Rome
conferr'd on him and in him
the whole Power over the World in the Capitol.

[p.10] Opposite the North Front of the House, at the Head of the Canal, is the Equestrian Statue of his late Majesty, in Armour.

The North Front of the House extends, with the Offices, 640 Feet in Breadth, having an open View, bounded by a Semi-Circle of Trees at some Miles distance.

Opposite the South Front was the Parterre, with the Statues of *Apollo* and the nine Muses, and two Orangeries; but this is alter'd to make room for a nobler Prospect.

The Statue of his present Majesty
is erected on a Corinthian Pillar, with this Inscription:

Georgio Augusto.

Dido's Cave

is an antique dark Stone Building, with this Inscription:

Speluncam Dido, dux & Trojanus, [ean]dem
Deveniunt...

[p.11] *In English thus:*

Repairing to the same dark Cave are seen
The *Trojan* Hero and the *Tyrian* Queen.

The Rotunda

is raised on Ionic Pillars on a gentle Rise, within is the Statue
of *Venus de Medicis,* gilt, on a Pedestal of blue Marble. The
Building is the Design of Sir *John Vanbrugh.* —The Views from
hence are inchanting.

The late Queen's Statue

is erected on four Ionic Columns, in a green Amphitheatre
laid out in the rural Way, with this Inscription:

Honori, Laudi, Virtuti Divæ Carolinæ.

To the Honour, Praise, and Virtue of the Divine *Caroline.*

The Sleeping Parlour

is placed in a close Wood where six Walks meet. It is a square
Building, with this Inscription:

Cum omnia sint in incerto, fave tibi.

[p.12] *Which is:*

Since all Things are uncertain, indulge thyself.

From hence you come into the great Avenue, where, on
the Right Hand, you have the Prospect of the Entrance to the

Page 50.

Temple of Modern Virtue.

Buckham delt. et 1750

Engraving by George Bickham from *The Beauties of Stow*

Gardens (mentioned before); and, on the Left, the Mansion-House, which, with the Additions now building, makes a grand Appearance.

The Witch-House.

Not far from the Witch-House is a House that formerly belonged to the Vicar; near this are placed on Pedestals, *Apollo* and the nine Muses round the Spring of *Helicon*.

The Temple of modern Virtue,
in Ruin.

The Temple of antient Virtue

is a Rotunda of the Doric Order by Mr. *Kent*; and on the Outside over each Door is this Motto:

Priscae Virtuti.

To antient Virtue.

[p.13] And in four Niches within, standing at full Length, are the four following Statues, viz.

1. Epaminondas,
with this Inscription:

Cujus a virtute, prudentia verecundia,
Thebanorum respublica
Libertatem simul & imperium,
Disciplinam bellicam, civilem & domesticam
Accepit;
Eoque amisso, perdidit.

That is;

From whose Valour, Prudence, and Moderation, the Republick of *Thebes* received both Liberty and Empire; its military, civil, and domestick Discipline; and, with him, lost them.

2. Lycurgus,
with this:

Qui summo cum consilio inventis legibus,
Omnemque contra corruptelam munitis optime,
Pater patriæ,
Libertatem firmissimam,
Et mores sanctissimos,
[p.14]Expulsa cum divitiis avaritia, luxuria, libidine,
In multa secula
Civibus suis instituit.

Thus translated:

Who having invented Laws with the greatest Wisdom, and most excellently fenced them against all Corruption, as a Father of his Country, instituted for his Countrymen the firmest Liberty and the soundest Morality, which endured for many Ages, he having, together with Riches, banished Avarice, Luxury, and Lust.

3. Socrates.

Qui corruptissima in civitate innocens,
Bonorum hortator, unici cultor DEI,
Ab inutili otio, & vanis disputationibus,
Ad officia vitæ, & societatis commoda,
Philosophiam avocavit,
Hominum sapientissimus.

That is:

Who being innocent in a most corrupt State, an Encourager of the Good, a Worshiper of one only God, as the wisest of Men reduced [p.15] Philosophy from useless Indolence, and vain Disputations, to the Duties of Life, and the Advantages of Society.

4. Homerus.

Qui poetarum princeps, idem & maximus,
Virtutis præco, & immortalitatis largitor
Divino carmine,
Ad pulcre audendum, & patiendum fortiter,
Omnibus notus gentibus, omnes incitat.

Thus rendered:

Who being the first of Poets, as he was the greatest, the Herald of Virtue, and Bestower of Immortality, known to all Nations, incites all, in a Divine Poem, honourably to dare, and resolutely to suffer.

Over one Door is this Inscription:

Charum esse civem, bene de republica mereri, laudari, coli, diligi, gloriosum est: metui vero, & in odio esse, invidiosum, detestabile, imbecillum, caducum.

Which is:

To be dear to our Country, to deserve well of the State, to be praised, honoured, and be- [p.16] loved, is glorious; but to be dreaded and hated is Matter of ill Will, detestable, weak, ruinous.

Over the other Door this:

Justitiam cole & pietatem, quæ cum sit magna in parentibus & propinquis, tum in patria maxima est. Ea vita via est in cœlum, & in hunc cœtum eorum, qui jam vixerunt.

In English thus:

Maintain Justice, and thy relative Duty; which, as it is great, when exercised toward our Parents and Kindred, so is greater toward our Country. That Life is the Way to Heaven, and to this Assembly of those who have already lived.

The Parish Church.

The Serpentine River,

at the Head of which is the Grotto, and on each Side two Pavillions, the one ornamented with Shells, as the other is with Pebbles and Flints broke to pieces. —The Grotto is furnished with a great Number of Looking-glasses both on the Walls and Cieling, all in artificial [p.17] Frames of Plaister-work, set with Shells and broken Flints—a Marble Statue of *Venus* on a Pedestal stuck with the same.

The Chinese-House

is situated in a Pond, and you enter it by a Bridge adorn'd with Chinese Vases, with Flowers in them. It is a square Building with four Lattices, and cover'd with Sail-cloth to preserve the Lustre of the Paintings; in it is a Chinese Lady as if asleep, her Hands covered by her Gown. In the Pond are the Figures of two Chinese Birds about the Size of a Duck, which move with the Wind as if alive. The Outside of the House is painted in the Taste of that Nation, by Mr. *Slater*, the Inside is India japann'd Work.

The Shell-Bridge,

which brings you into the Elysian Fields, which well deserve that Name; where stands

The Temple of Worthies;

a Building cut into Niches, wherein are placed the following Bustos. The first is

Mr. Pope,
with no Inscription.

[p.18] Sir Thomas Gresham,
Who, by the honourable Profession of a Merchant, having

enrich'd himself, and his Country, for carrying on the Commerce of the World built the Royal Exchange.

Ignatius Jones,

Who, to adorn his Country, introduc'd and rival'd the Greek and Roman Architecture.

John Milton,

Whose sublime and unbounded Genius equal'd a Subject that carried him beyond the Limits of the World.

William Shakespear,

Whose excellent Genius open'd to him the whole Heart of Man, all the Mines of Fancy, all the Stores of Nature; and gave him Power, beyond all other Writers, to move, astonish, and delight Mankind.

John Lock,

Who, best of all Philosophers, understood the Powers of the human Mind; the Nature, End, and Bounds of Civil Government; and, [p.19] with equal Courage and Sagacity, refuted the slavish Systems of usurp'd Authority over the Rights, the Consciences, or the Reason of Mankind.

Sir Isaac Newton,

Whom the God of Nature made to comprehend his Works; and, from simple Principles, to discover the Laws never known before, and to explain the Appearance never understood, of this Stupendous Universe.

Sir Fra. Bacon, *Lord Verulam*,

Who by the Strength and Light of a superior Genius, rejecting vain Speculation, and fallacious Theory, taught to pursue Truth, and improve Philosophy by the certain Method of Experiment.

In the Niche of a Pyramid is placed a Mercury, with these Words subscribed:

—Campos Ducit ad Elysios.

—Leads to the Elysian Fields.

And below this Figure is fix'd a Square of black Marble, with the following Lines:

[p.20] Hic manus ob patriam pugnando vulnera passi,
Quique pii vates, & Phœbo digna locuti,
Inventas aut qui vitam excoluere per artes,
Quique sui memores alios fecere merendo.

Thus translated:

Here are the Bands, who for their Country bled,
And Bards, whose pure and sacred Verse is read:
Those, who, by Arts invented, Life improv'd,
And, by their Merits, made their Mem'ries lov'd.

King Alfred,

The mildest, justest, most beneficent of Kings; who drove out the Danes, secur'd the Seas, protected Learning, establish'd Juries, crush'd Corruption, guarded Liberty, and was the Founder of the English Constitution.

Edward, Prince of Wales,

The Terror of Europe, the Delight of England; who preserv'd, unalter'd, in the Height of Glory and Fortune, his natural Gentleness and Modesty.

[p.21] Queen Elizabeth,

Who confounded the Projects, and destroy'd the Power that threaten'd to oppress the Liberties of Europe; took off the Yoke of Ecclesiastical Tyranny; restored Religion from the Corruptions of Popery; and by a wise, a moderate, and a popular Government, gave Wealth, Security, and Respect to England.

King William 3ᵈ.

Who by his Virtue and Constancy, having saved his Country from a foreign Master, by a bold and generous Enterprize, preserv'd the Liberty and Religion of Great Britain.

Sir Walter Raliegh,

A valiant Soldier, and an able Statesman; who endeavouring to rouze the Spirit of his Master, for the Honour of his Country, against the Ambition of Spain, fell a Sacrifice to the Influence of that Court, whose Arms he had vanquish'd, and whose Designs he oppos'd.

Sir Francis Drake,

Who, through many Perils, was the first of Britons that adventur'd to sail round the Globe; [p.22] and carried into unknown Seas and Nations the Knowledge and Glory of the English Name.

John Hampden,

Who with great Spirit, and consumate Abilities, begun a noble Opposition to an arbitrary Court, in Defence of the Liberties of his Country; supported them in Parliament, and died for them in the Field.

Sir John Barnard,
with no Inscription.

On the Backside of this Building is the following Monument, with this Inscription:

To The Memory
of
Signor Fido,
an Italian of good Extraction;
who came into England,
not to bite us, like most of his Countrymen,
but to gain an honest Livelyhood.
He hunted not after Fame,
yet acquir'd it;
regardless of the Praise of his Friends,
but most sensible of their Love.
[p.23] Tho' he liv'd amongst the Great,

he neither learnt nor flatter'd any Vice.
He was no Bigot,
Tho' he doubted of none of the 39 Articles.
And, if to follow Nature,
and to respect the Laws of Society,
be Philosophy,
he was a perfect Philosopher; ·
a faithful Friend,
an agreeable Companion,
a loving Husband,
distinguish'd by a numerous Offspring,
all which he liv'd to see take good Courses.
In his old Age he retir'd
to the House of a Clergyman in the Country,
where he finish'd his earthly Race,
and died an Honour and an Example to the whole Species.
Reader,
this Stone is guiltless of Flattery;
for he to whom it is inscrib'd
was not a Man
but a

Grey-Hound.

The Temple of Liberty

is a large Gothic Building of red Stone, 70 Feet high, on the Brow of the Hill; round which [p.24] are placed the seven Statues mentioned before.

On the Left Hand stands my Lady's Temple, but not finish'd. It commands a beautiful Prospect over the Country.

The Palladian Bridge;

where is a Collection of antique Bustoes of Marble: The Roof, on the Side facing the Water, is supported by Ionic Columns; the Backside of it by an Alto-Relievo of the four Quarters of the World bringing their Products to *Britannia*.

Here are likewise painted by Mr. *Slater*, Sir *Walter Raleigh*, with a Map of *Virginia* in his Hand; and Sir *William Penn*, holding a Book, stiled, *The Laws of Pensylvania*.

The Imperial Closet

is a Room of a Cubic Form, and in it are the three following Figures, painted at full Length, by Mr. *Slater*.

Imp. Titus Cæs. Vespasian.

with his Saying over his Head,

Diem perdidi—I have lost a Day.

[p.25] Imp. N. Trajan. Cæs. Au.

with his Saying,

Pro me: si merear, in me.

For me: but, if I deserve it, against me.

Imp. Marcus Aurelius
Cæsar Antoninus.

with his Saying:

Ita regnes imperator, ut privatus regi te velis.

So govern, when an Emperor, as, if a private
Person, you would desire to be governed.

This brings you upon the great Terrace-Walk, which is near 3000 Feet long.

The Temple of Friendship;

a noble Structure, of the Doric Order. On the Outside is this Motto:

Amicitiæ S. —Sacred to Friendship.

Within is painted, on the Cieling, *Britannia*, with some other
Figures; one holds a Label, [p.26] with these Words, *The Reign
of K. Edward 3.* another a Scroll with, *The Reign of Q. Elizabeth*;
and another with, *The Reign of ... the ...* the rest being cover'd
with her Mantle: And several other Ornaments in Painting, by
Mr. *Slater*.

Also in this are the following ten Bustoes of my Lord and
his illustrious Friends, viz. the Prince of *Wales*—Earls of
Westmoreland, Chesterfield, and *Marchmont*—Lords *Cobham,
Gower,* and *Bathurst*—*Richard Greenville, William Pitt,* and *George
Lyttleton,* Esqrs.

The Pebble Alcove
is a neat Recess, and very artfully imbellished with Pebbles; his
Lordship's Arms are perform'd with the same, and display'd
in proper Colours.

Congreve's Monument
is an Urn, which, with great Art, expresses the Genius of the
Man; and at the Top of it is placed a Monkey, beholding
himself in a Mirror, and under him this Writing:

Vitæ imitatio,
Consuetudin[is] speculum,
Comœdia.

[p.27] *That is:*

Comedy is the Imitation of Life, and the Glass of Fashion.

The Poet's Effigies, lying in a careless Posture, has the
following Inscription:

Ingenio
Acri, faceto, expolito,
Moribusque
Urbanis, candidis, facillimis,

Gulielmi Congreve,
Hoc
Qualecunque desiderii sui
[Sol]amen simul &
Monumentum
Posuit COBHAM
1736.

Thus translated:

In the Year 1736, COBHAM erected this poor Consolation for, as well as Monument of, his Loss of the piercing, elegant, polished Wit, and civilized, candid, most unaffected Manners, of WILLIAM CONGREVE.

F I N I S.

William Gilpin (1724 – 1804)

A Dialogue upon the Gardens of
the Right Honourable the Lord Viscount Cobham,
at Stow in Buckinghamshire (1748)

Encouraged by the success of his *Description of the Gardens*, Seeley embarked on a fresh venture. In 1747 he had printed a sermon which the young William Gilpin preached in Buckingham, and in the following year he published Gilpin's *Dialogue upon the Gardens*, in which two friends walk the usual tourist route round the gardens, arguing about the merits of everything they see. Seeley's intention is clear. He wanted a commentary on the gardens as a companion piece to his factual *Description*, and this is what the *Dialogue* provided. A second edition, slightly amended, came out in 1749, and a third followed in 1751, when the dialogue was changed to narrative. All were published anonymously, but there is no doubt of Gilpin's authorship.

But over and above its importance in Stowe's tourist literature, the *Dialogue* is valuable as evidence of the youthful Gilpin's taste for the picturesque, though he did not use the word itself for another twenty years. The characters of the two friends are indicated by their names: Callophilus is a lover of natural beauty which has been improved by art, whereas Polypthon, habitually grudging and critical, dislikes artificial decoration in a natural setting. In the most eloquent of his speeches he enthusiastically describes the rugged natural beauty of northern Britain. Their characters are not rigidly maintained. Both respond sympathetically to aesthetic and philosophic features of the gardens.

For reasons of space the text of the *Dialogue* has reluctantly been left out of this collection. But it has been reprinted elsewhere in recent years and can be found in a volume published by the Augustan Reprint Society, ed. J.D. Hunt (Los Angeles, 1976); in *The Gardens of Stowe*, Vol. 16 in the series *The English Landscape Garden* (New York, 1982); and three substantial excerpts in *The Genius of the Place*, ed. J.D. Hunt and P. Willis (London, 1975 and 1988).

Keeper's Lodge in the Park.

P. 60

Castle

Bickham According to Act 1750.

Engraving by George Bickham
from *The Beauties of Stow*

Benton Seeley (1716 – 1795)

Views of the Temples and other ornamental Buildings in the Gardens (1750)

Yet another of Seeley's projects was to publish a collection of views of the garden buildings. These varied in size, many being quite small and appearing six to an octavo page. Though crude, they were accurate enough to remind visitors of what they had seen on their tour of the gardens, and in time, as worn-out plates had to be replaced, the quality of the engravings improved. They were on sale at the New Inn, like Seeley's other publications, and were the equivalent of the picture books which visitors nowadays buy in the shop at the end of their tour of a country house.

The whole set of ten plates is reproduced here. Five were engraved by George Vertue and five by G. Vandergucht, all taken from drawings made by Seeley himself. More information was engraved on the plates at each reprinting, to include such things as the plate numbers and the names of the engravers; and at least two of the engravings, those of the Rotunda and the Grecian Temple, were cleaned off and re-engraved when the buildings were altered. The engravings of the buildings reproduced in the following pages are all thought to be in their first state, though possibly not from their first printing.

Several of the plates are dated "May 1 1750", and the Views must have been on sale soon afterwards, for Sanderson Miller noted that he had purchased "Seely's Prints of Stowe" on July 10th. So by the summer of 1750 three of Seeley's Stowe publications were available in Buckingham and London: the Description for sixpence, the Dialogue for a shilling, and the Views for two shillings and sixpence. All were octavo, and, bound up together with a combined title page, they cost five shillings. It is clear that Seeley's business activities were steadily expanding, though the flowery pen-work in his dedication of the Views is a reminder of his humble beginnings as a country writing-master.

It was Stowe which launched Benton Seeley's personal career and his family's prosperity, as it also launched a number of other successful careers, including those of William Pitt and 'Capability' Brown.

TO:

The Right Honourable the

Lord Viscount Cobham

These VIEWS of

Temples, and other Ornamental Buildings, in

The Gardens at Stow,

Are humbly Dedicated by his

Lordship's

Obliged & most obed.t Servant,

B. Seeley.

148

Plate I.

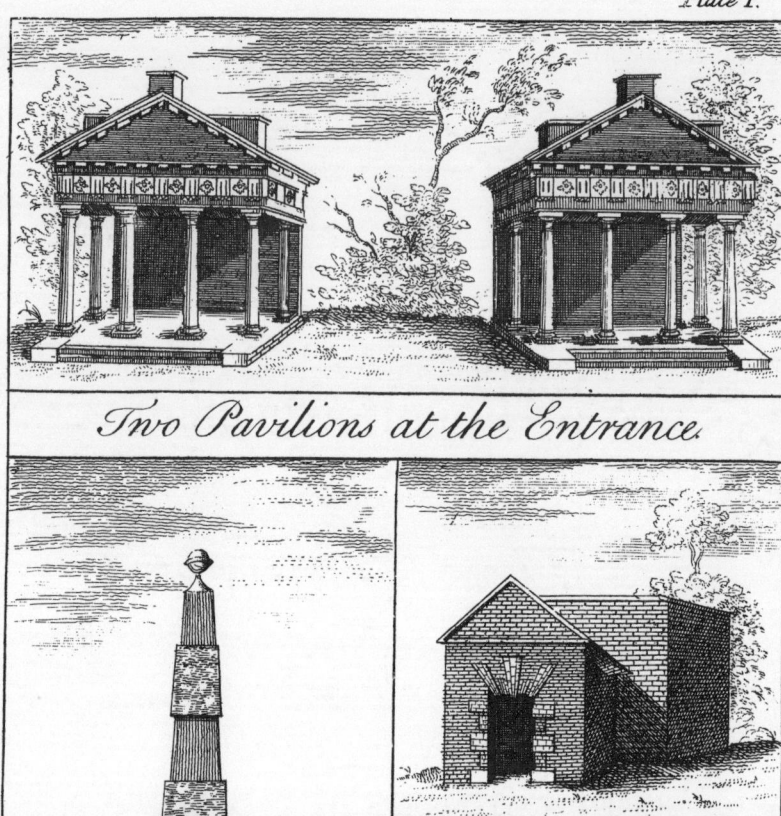

Two Pavilions at the Entrance.

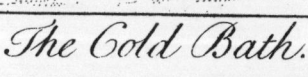

The Cold Bath.

The Obelisk.   *The Hermitage.*

Publish'd according to Act of Parliament May 1.1750.   *B. Seeley. delin.*

Publish'd according to Act of Parliament. 1750.

An Artificial Peice of Rock-work.

The Temple dedicated to Venus.

B. Seeley delin.

An Egyptian Pyramid.

The Belvidere.

Publish'd according to Act of Parliament. 1750.

Two Pavilions at the Entrance to the Park.

St Augustine's Cave.   The Temple of Bacchus.

Couchers Obelisk.   Nelsons Seat.

B. seeley delin.

151

Dido's Cave.

The Rotunda.

King George 2.

Queen Caroline.

Publish'd according to Act of Parliament May 1.1750.

B. Seeley delin.

Publish'd according to Act of Parliam.t 1750.

The Sleeping Parlour

The Witch House

The Temple of Modern Virtue.

The Temple of Antient Virtue.

The Shell Bridge.

B. Seeley delin.

Publish'd according to Act of Parliament 1750.

The Temple of British Worthies.

The Chinese House.   The Temple of Contemplation.

B. Seeley delin.

The Grotto.

154

The Grecian Temple.

The Lady's Temple.

Capt. Grenville's
Monument.

The Keeper's Lodge in the Park.

B. Seeley delin.

Publish'd according to Act of Parliament, 1750.

To preserve the Memory of her Husband,
Ann Viscountefs Cobham,
Caused this Pillar to be erected in the Year 1747

B. .... *Publish'd according to Act of Parliament May 1.1750.*

The Gothic Temple.

The Palladian Bridge.

B. Seeley delin.   Publish'd according to act of Parliament. 1750.

The Temple of Friendship.

The Pebble Alcove.

The Imperial Closet

Congreve's Monument.

B. Seeley delin.   Publish'd according to act of Parliament, 1750.

J. d. C.

Les
CHARMES
de
STOW:
ou
DESCRIPTION
de
La belle Maison de Plaisance
de
Mylord COBHAM.
par
J. d. C.

à LONDRES,
chès J. NOURSE, 1748.

This is the full text on the title page of J. d. C's book, which cost one shilling. It was noted by its main title in the booklist of the *Gentleman's Magazine* for June 1749, and in the same month the booklist of the *British Magazine* contained both its title and subtitle, adding the phrase, "avec une traduction angloise a Cote". But no copy with an accompanying English translation has yet been discovered—in fact, only a single copy of this book has so far come to light, bound in with a pirated edition of the *Description of the Gardens* and a copy of Bickham's *Beauties of Stow*, both of 1750.

Clearly Bickham knew of *Les Charmes*, for he translated its title and used it for his own book; and several passages in *Les Charmes* are so similar to Gilpin's *Dialogue* that the two must be related. The book's author, "J. d. C.", has not been identified. Its publisher, J. Nourse, certainly produced a number of titles in foreign languages, and a pamphlet in French, addressed to a young woman and written in the epistolary convention of the day, was presumably directed to a French audience. It is tempting to cite it as evidence of growing French interest in Stowe's gardens a dozen years before Rousseau's critical comments in *La Nouvelle Héloïse*, but no hypothesis can be safely based on a single copy. *Les Charmes* raises a number of unanswered questions.

Les Charmes de Stow
(1748)

MADEMOISELLE,

Enfin j'ai vû *Stow*, cette petite *merveille* do nos jours, & le lieu le plus enchanté de toute *l'Angleterre!* Il n'est point de *Voïageur* tant soit peu Connoisseur & Curieux, qui venant à *Londres* n'aille voir *Bleinheim*, & surtout *Stow*, comme étant tout ce que ce riche Pays a de plus brillant & de plus magnifique. Je fus frappé [p.6] de la majesté du Chateau de *Blenheim*; & si effectivement je le trouvai plus *somptueux* que *gracieux*, je ne laissai pas d'admirer la beauté de ses Appartemens, la richesse de ses Ornemens & de ses Peintures, & surtout la belle *Gallerie*, qui renferme la *Bibliothèque* du Duc de *Malborough*. D'ailleurs je fus charmé du riant coup d'oeil, qu'offrent & le *Pont*, & la *Riviére*, & la *Colonne* érigée à l'honeur du grand *Malborough*, de même que tout le *Paysage* des environs. Mais tout cela n'égale point les beautés de l'incomparable *Stow*. J'avoüe que le *Bois* fameux du Chevalier *Jérémie Sembrock*, à *Gubbins*, dans la Comté de *Hertford*, est digne de l'admiration d'un *Voïageu*r, & que l'on y trouve *en petit* plusieurs conformités avec *Stow*. Par example; figurez vous une vaste Colline toute ombragée d'une Forêt de Chênes, & dans laquelle on a pratiqué une infinité d'allées en tout sens, & couvertes du plus beau gravier. On y trouve tantôt une *Grote* agréablement ornée, & où se fait entendre le doux murmure d'une *Cascade*, entourée d'arbres touffus; tantôt on arrive à une grande *Place* embellie *d'Orangers* & de *Statues,* & d'un beau *Cabinet* dont toutes les fenêtres présentent d'agréables vuës; tantôt a un magnifique *Bassin* [p.7] orné de *Pyramides* vertes, *d'Orangers*, de *Statuës*, & entouré d'allées d'une très grande étenduë; tantôt à une espéce de *Cercle de Verdure*, tout couvert des arbres mêmes de la Forêt, mais éclaircis avec tant d'art & de goût, que le coup d'oeil en est ravissant; en un mot, la beauté des Allées dont les hayes vives sont d'une hauteur étonnante, la fraicheur des ombrages, la riante variété des Perspectives, la richesse des ornemens, & le goût peu commun qui régne dans toute la distribution, & le choix des diverses parties de cette charmante Retraite, en font un *Bois* presque unique dans son espéce, & un séjour délicieux. Mais quelque admirable que soit *Gubbins*, il faut qu'il cède le pas à *Stow*, qui est incomparablement plus magnifique & plus agréable. J'en suis si épris, que semblable aux tendres *Amans* qui parlent sans cesse des attrais de leurs *Iris*, je ne puis me lasser de raconter à tout le Monde, de combien de charmes *Stow* est enrichi; & que j'ose même vous en entretenir uniquement, *Mademoiselle*, dans cette *Lettre*. Cela n'est pas autrement *galant* je l'avouë; mais il l'est toujours de se conformer au goût de la Personne à qui l'on parle, & vous m'avez parû souhaiter extrémement, que je vous donnâsse une [p.8] *Description* un peu détaillée du fameux *Stow*, dont on vous a dit tant de merveilles. Après tout, *Mademoiselle*, ma *Lettre* ne sera pas tout à fait destituée de ces traits que l'usage appelle *Galanterie*, & qui sont comme une sorte de *tribut*, que notre *Sexe* est dans la douce obligation de payer au *vôtre*, comme à des *Souveraines* auxquelles la *Nature* de concert avec *l'Habitude* soumettent nos Coeurs, de tems immémorial, & presque sans exception.

Pardonnez moi cette petite digression *Mademoiselle*; & permettez que je me livre de tems en tems aux caprices de mon *Imagination*, en traitant un sujet où elle semble avoir épuisé tous ses trésors: et d'ailleurs je suis présentement au milieu du Peuple le plus *libre* de *l'Europe*, dans le Pays qui est le centre & l'azile de la *Liberté*, où l'on peut tout dire & tout publier, & où chacun est maitre de donner un libre essor à ses pensées, quelque absurdes, quelque chimériques, quelques foles qu'elles puissent être! L'heureuse Nation que la Nation *Angloise!* Elle a brisé les fers dont presque tout le reste du Genre-humain est captivé; elle seule est un vrai Peuple *d'Hommes!*

[p.9] Réjouissez vous *Mademoiselle*, nous voici à *Stow*. J'oubliois pourtant de vous dire, que la route qui y mène d'*Oxford*, est très mauvaise; ce sont 4 à 5 heures de chemin où l'on ne rencontre presque que de vastes bruyères, des lieux secs & raboteux, & une espèce de solitude toute propre à favoriser l'audace des Elèves de *Mercure*, & à servir de *Théatre* à leurs dangéreux exploits. Mais rassurez vous, il y a très

longtems qu'ils n'y ont commis aucune insulte; & il ne paroit
pas qu'ils y soient craint par les habitans.

On apperçoit de *trois milles* de loin la belle *Maison de Plaisance
de Stow.* Elle est sur une hauteur, & elle présente toute sa façade
en plein dans ce point de vuë; mais un peu au dèla, on ne la
voit plus que lors qu'on en est tout proche. Ce coup d'oeil est
des plus surprenans; car au sortir d'une route peu gracieuse,
vous appercevez tout d'un coup une longue *Avenuë,* au bout
de laquelle s'élève un bel *Obélisque,* qui laisse entrevoir une
Maison magnifique, placée sur le haut d'une Colline, &
entourée de mille objets qui en augmentent l'agrément. On
entre dans ce charmant [p.10] *Jardin,* par un *Perron* qui conduit
sur la superbe *Terrasse,* qui règne en travers tout le long du
Jardin, & qui est couverte d'Arbres alignés qui forment une Allée
à perte de vuë. De chaque coté du *Perron,* l'on trouve un *Pavillon*
très propre & de fort bon goût, peint à *fresque,* & représentant
l'un, l'avanture de *Dorinde* & de *Sylvio,* & l'autre celle de
Myrtille & *d'Amarillis,* tirées du *Pastor Fido.* Ces *Pavillons* font
face à la *Maison,* & à *l'Obélisque* qui se trouve placé au bas de la
Terrasse, dans une magnifique *Piéce d'eau,* & qui sert à en
distribuer par des tuïaux de plomb en divers endroits éloignés.
Rien de plus agréable à la vuë que ce Vaste *Etang,* qui d'un coté
tombe par *trois* belles *Cascades,* sous des *Mazures* artificielles,
dans un petit *Lac* tout entouré de gazon & de verdure, & qui
sur la droite communique sous un joli *Pont* à un long bras de
riviére, qui a sa source sous un très beau *Pont* de pierres, dont
nous parlerons dans la suite. Représentez vous maintenant &
cette *Avenuë,* & cette *Terrasse* qui la croise, & ces *Pavillons,* & ce
grand *Obélisque,* & cet *Etang,* & cette *Maison* magnifique sur le
haut de la Colline, & ces *Mazures* artificielles couvertes de roc
& de Mousse, [p.11] ces *Cascades,* cet autre *Lac,* la *Riviére,* ces
Ponts, & mille & mille Arbres arrangés de toute façon; & vous
conviendrez que ce début est tout à fait charmant, & qu'il
n'annonce pas moins que des *Merveilles!*

Mais remontons sur la *Terrasse,* & tirons *à gauche,* pour nous
rendre dabord au *Temple* de *Vénus.* A ce mot, *Mademoiselle,*
vous rougissez, le Coeur vous bat, & vôtre aimable pudeur
sent quelque allarme! Mais de grace ne vous effrayez point.

Boycott Buildings.

Two of these Pavilions at the Entrance.

Two of these Pavilions at the Entrance of y Fort.

Engraving by George Bickham from *The Beauties of Stow*

Mylord *Cobham* est un Seigneur trop modeste, pour avoir donné entrée dans son *Paradis terrestre* à quoi que ce soit qui pût choquer les bienséances, ou blesser la délicatesse du *Beau-Sexe*. Ce *Temple de Vénus* est un petit Edifice de pierres de taille, d'un très bon goût, & qui ne contient qu'une seule Chambre toute ornée de Peintures *galantes* à la vérité, mais néanmoins nullement *obscénes*. Vous sentez bien que ce *Temple* ne peut représenter que des Avantures *amoureuses*; aussi y voit on la belle *Hellinore*, qui aïant quitté son vieux Epoux, & errant dans les Forêts rencontre une Troupe de *Satyres*, avec lesquels elle se met à danser; l'inconsolable *Malbecco* la découvre en fin, & l'observe de [p.12] derriére un Arbre, couchée au milieu de ces hideux Galands alors tous endormis; il en approche en tremblant, & sollicite sa fugitive Epouse de le suivre; mais elle lui ordonne de se retirer, le menaçant de réveiller ses redoutables Rivaux, & de l'en faire déchirer s'il ne se retire incessament; *Malbecco* obéit, & tombe en démence. Toutes ces peintures, leur dessein, leur coloris, l'execution, tout cela part d'une habile main. J'aurois seulement souhaité, qu'au lieu de tant de *Satyres* dont ce *Temple* est défiguré, l'on y eût dépeint des *Amans* moins lascifs; & que *Cupidon* y parût sous une forme plus digne de lui, & tel qu'il règne parmi les honnêtes gens. Mais en tout cas, *Mademoiselle*, on peut se contenter de voir ce *Temple* voluptueux, par dehors, & sans y entrer.

En continuant à parcourir la *Terrasse*, l'on arrive enfin à un *Edifice* très massif, de forme *Cubique* & *Pyramidale*, qui la borne d'une maniére très convenable, & auquel on monte par une douce rampe. La longueur extraordinaire de la *Terrasse* exigeoit sans doute que cet *Edifice* fut lourd & haut; car sans cela il n'auroit pas bien figuré dans l'eloignement. De là vous [p.13] avez la vuë sur quantité de champs & de prairies, dont le diversité fait un très agréable effet; & cet endroit tout *champêtre* semble fait exprès, pour servir de *contraste* aux merveilles que l'Art offre dans la suite.

Dabord c'est *Belvidere* que l'on rencontre, & dont tout l'usage se réduit à servir à quantité de *Points de vuë* différens qui y aboutissent, au travers de mille Allées charmantes. On trouve tout près de là deux *Statuës* qui n'expriment pas mal une *Lute* à la *Romaine*; & vis à vis du *Temple de Vénus*, on entre dans un nouvel *Edifice*, qui renferme diverses *Statuës* revêtuës de *drapperie*, à l'antique. Assés près delà s'élève une énorme *Pyramide*, faite de pierres de taille, & toute composée de *Marches* qui vont toujours en se retrécissant jusques au Sommet; elles couvrent en voute une *Chambre* assés basse, & qui est toute vuide, ne pouvant servir que de *Caveau* pour les *Morts*. Vous ne sauriez croire combien cette *Pyramide* est heureusement située, pour figurer dans divers Points de vuë, & dans l'éloignement; cela sent un peu *l'Egypte*, où il y avoit des *Pyramides* si majestueuses.

[p.14] En prenant toujours sur *la gauche*, on perd tout d'un coup la vuë du *Jardin*, & de toutes ses beautés que vous dérobent des *hayes vives*, & quantité d'Arbrisseaux. Cela est ménagé avec beaucoup d'art; comme les *Ombres* dans un *Tableau*, & les *Pauses* en *Musique*. Cependant on est en quelque sorte dédomagé de la privation de ces riantes *Perspectives*, par la vuë du *Parc* & du *Paysage* qui l'environne, demême que par celle de la belle *Statuë Equestre* du Roi, qui est posée au bout d'un grand *Etang*, vis à vis de la Façade de derriére de la *Maison*, & qui fait un très bel effet dans cet endroit là. De ce même point, l'on apperçoit sur *la droite* dans l'éloignement, le beau *Temple de l'ancienne Vertu*, & en s'y acheminant on rentre dans les belles Allées.

Le *Siège de Nelson* se présente dabord. C'est un très joli Edifice, fort petit, bien peint, & dont les *Inscriptions* expliquent le dessein. Mais *le Temple de Bacchus* mérite une plus grande attention; & l'on ne manque guéres de s'y asseoir quelques momens, soit pour y reprendre haleine, soit pour en admirer la Peinture qui est très curieuse. On voit sur les murs [p.15] le *Triomphe de l'Yvresse & de la Joie*; & sur le *Plat-fonds* le Dieu *Bacchus* d'une grosseur énorme. Les *petites Figures* sont excellentes, de même que les *deux Vases* qui sont peints sur l'un des murs. La vuë est charmante tout autour de ce bel Edifice, & tout semble concourir à y inspirer de la joie. Au sortir de là, une petite Allée assés sombre & détournée vous conduit à la *Grote de Didon* si fameuse dans *l'Enéide de Virgile*. Cette *Grote* ne pouvoit être mieux placée que proche du

Temple de Bacchus; l'un conduit naturellement à l'autre. On y voit le *pieux Enée* aux piés de sa belle *Carthaginoise*, peints l'un & l'autre d'une maniére ingénieuse, & à leurs cotés, *deux* gentils *Amours* qui tiennent des *torches* allumées & réunies, & qui sont admirablement bien représentés. A cette vuë, *Mademoiselle*, mon Coeur frémit de dépit contre cet *infidèle* Prince *Troïen*, qui passionément aimé d'une *Reine* douée de mille charmes, la paya de la plus noire ingratitude, l'abandonna, & lui causa la mort! Je fus fâché, pour l'honneur de mon *Sexe*, de voir revivre ici une Avanture que je voudrois qui fut ensevelie pour jamais dans l'oubli; ainsi que devoit aussi l'être [p.16] celle de la *Matrone d'Ephèse*, pour l'honneur du *vôtre*. Mais remarquez en passant, combien Mylord *Cobham* est de vos Amis; puis qu'il a êu soin de ne placer nulle part, parmi tant d'ornemens si variés dont il a embelli ce séjour délicieux, aucun Monument qui pût désobliger le *Beau-sexe*, tandis qu'il n'a pas eû les mêmes attentions pour *le nôtre*.

Un *Edifice* majestueux se présente près de là, c'est la *Rotonde*. Il n'y a aucun Bâtiment de pierres dans tout le *Jardin*, qui fasse un meilleur effet que celui ci, quant à la *Perspective*. D'un coté tous les *embellissemens* de *l'Art* s'offrent à la vuë; de l'autre un vaste *Théatre*; ici c'est un *Vallon* arrosé d'une *eau* claire & pure, & où se jouent quantité de *Cygnes* & de *Canards sauvages*; là une belle *Colonne*, sur laquelle est élevée *la Statuë du feu Roi*; & tout autour une Troupe de *Nymphes* & de *Sylvains* qui se divertissent à l'ombre. Ce Coup d'oeil est tout à fait riant.

Le *Temple du Sommeil* vous ouvre ses portes, à quelque distance delà; comme pour [p.17] vous tirer d'un trop grand effort d'admiration, & vous donner le loisir de reprendre de nouvelles forces, afin de pouvoir parcourir plus aisément le reste des beautés de cette demeure enchantée. Ce *Temple* est situé au fond d'une *Solitude* ménagée avec tout l'art imaginable, au milieu d'un petit Bois sombre & frais, éloigné de tout bruit, & ne respirant pour ainsi dire que le *repos*. L'Edifice est de pierres de taille, & ne comprend qu'une *Salle* médiocre, où de commodes *Canapés* vous invitent au *Sommeil*, & où se trouvent de très aimables peintures à *fresque* sur tous les Murs. J'oubliois de vous dire, qu'avant que de s'y rendre, on passe auprès de *l'Hermitage de St. Augustin*, qui est singulier dans son genre, n'étant fait que de *mousse* & de *racines d'Arbres* admirablement bien mêlés ensemble, & n'aïant pour tout ornement *qu'une Chaise de Bois*, un *Lit de Paille*, & diverses *Inscriptions* sur des tablettes, en *vers Monastiques*. Voïez combien on a eû soin de ménager partout des *ombres* dans ce magnifique Tableau; car après avoir été ravi par des Objets brillans & enchanteurs, vous en rencontrez tout de suite de plus doux & de [p.18] plus simples. Cela marque un *Goût* exquis dans le *Génie* qui préside ici.

Du *Temple du Sommeil* on vous conduit fort naturellement à *l'Antre Magique*, car la *Nuit* est la Mère de la *Nécromancie*. C'est ici une petite *Maison de Planches*, consacrée à la *Magie*, au *Sortilège*, & à *l'Astrologie*, dont toutes les figures, les opérations, & les artifices sont peints très ingénieusement, & très délicatement sur les Parois, de même qu'une infinité de *Phantômes* hideux & grotesques. On n'a pas manqué d'y placer aussi quelque part le fameux *Trépié* des *Sybilles*. Mais laissons là le *Tartare*, & passons aux *Champs Elisées*.

Dabord, c'est le *Temple de l'ancienne Vertu* qui se présente. Les plus Sages *Législateurs*, les plus sensés *Philosophes*, les plus excellens *Poètes*, & les plus illustres *Capitaines* en font tout l'ornement. On y trouve un *Lycurgue*, un *Socrate*, un *Homère*, & un *Epaminondas*, dont les *Bustes* sont placés dans chaque Mur du *Temple*. Ce choix est assurément très bien fondé; & il seroit difficile de trouver dans l'Antiquité, de plus grands hommes dans chacun [p.19] de ces genres, que ces *quatre Héros*. Une singularité que l'on remarque ici avec beaucoup de plaisir, c'est que les *Marches* de pierre qui conduisent à la *Porte* de ce *Temple* sont fort *étroites*, de même que la *Porte*; pour insinuer sans doute que l'on n'y entre pas *facilement*. Une autre chose bien remarquable, c'est que tout proche de ce *Temple*, il y a une *Masure artificielle*, qui *contraste* admirablement bien avec ce bel *Edifice* qui est tout *neuf*; & voici la clé de l'énigme. Ce *Temple* représente l'état florissant de *l'ancienne Vertu*, que rien n'a pû encore ni *envieillir* ni *détruire*, & qui brave les tems & les siècles; & ces *Masures*, & la *Vieille Statuë* qui en est proche, sont destinées à nous montrer *la fragilité* & la *caducité* de la *Vertu moderne*, qui est *décrépite* presque dès sa *naissance*. D'où l'on peut tirer cette belle *Moralité*; c'est que *la Gloire fondée sur le vrai mérite existe toujours*, tandis que *la réputation qui n'a d'autre fondement que les frivoles applaudissemens de la Multitude, s'évanouit aisément*. Cela est très ingénieux & très bien pensé.

De là, l'on se rend à la plus charmante *Grote* que l'on puisse imaginer. Il n'y a point [p.20] *d'Etranger* qui n'en soit enchanté. Figurez vous un petit *Edifice* tout formé de coquillages de *nacre de perles*, arrangés avec un art infini, & une patience de *Pénélope*; dont l'intérieur est composé d'une *Salle*, & de *deux Cabinets*, ornés d'une façon qui éblouit & qui charme! Ce sont partout des *glaces de Miroir* enchassées dans la *nacre*, & qui multiplient les *perspectives* du *Jardin*, & vôtre propre *Figure*, une infinité de fois. De chaque coté de cette riante *Grote*, est un petit *Temple*, soutenu, l'un de *quatre Colonnes torses*, l'autre de *quatre Colonnes droites*, toutes composées de même que leurs *Dômes*, de Coquillages de *nacre*, de tout ordre & de toute couleur; ce qui fait un effet ravissant! Et pour comble d'agrément & d'ornement, il sort du pié de cette *Grote* un aimable *ruisseau*, que l'on nomme *la petite Riviére*, & qui serpente au milieu de toute cette délicieuse contrée, qui porte à si juste titre le nom de *Champs Elisées*.

Une *Loge* tout à fait curieuse s'offre dans ce Voisinage; c'est la *Maison Chinoise*. Elle est de *bois*, & soutenüe sur quelques *pilotis*, au milieu de la *Riviére*. Ce n'est presque qu'une grande *Cage*, ou un petit *Cabinet*. On ne [p.21] peut rien imaginer de plus ingénieux, que la maniére dont on y a disposé les ornemens à *la Chinoise*. Ce sont tout autant de pièces de rapport, mais qui semblent avoir été faites exprès pour la place que l'Art leur fait occuper. Les *Fenêtres* sont faites d'un *Canevas* fin, qui laisse également une libre entrée au Jour & à l'Air. J'ai vû chés Mr. *Batman* tout proche de *Windsor*, une très jolie *Maison* bâtie à la *Chinoise*, mais incomparablement plus grande, & dans un goût tout différent.

De la *Loge Chinoise* on passe au *Temple du Mérite Britannique*. C'est un *Edifice* d'un goût singulier, sans toit & sans portes, bâti en quart de Cercle, & n'aiant qu'un seul mur, dans lequel sont enchassées les *Têtes* des plus *grands Hommes* que *l'Angleterre* ait

Engraving by George Bickham from *The Beauties of Stow*

produit. Ils sont ici en grand nombre; & c'est là une gloire que peu de Nations peuvent partager avec celle-ci. On y voit des *Philosophes*, un *Boyle*, un *Newton*, un *Locke*; des *Poètes*, un *Shakespear*, un *Dryden*, un *Milton*, un *Pope*; des *Magistrats*, un *Bacon*, &c. En un mot, cet aspect est tout à fait vénérable, & il inspire une sorte d'admiration & de respect! Tout [p.22] près de là se trouve *le Temple de la Contemplation*, qui est aussi un *Edifice* de pierres de taille, extrémement conforme à sa destination, étant construit & placé de façon à favoriser la *Méditation* & le *Recueillement*; & certes le souvenir de tous les Grands-Hommes que l'on vient d'admirer, ne peut que plonger dans une douce rêverie, & qu'exciter à la *Réflexion* sur leurs différens *Mérites*. C'est ainsi que rien n'est oublié ici, de tout ce qui peut contribuer à réunir *l'Utile* & *l'Agréable*.

Un peu plus loin l'on monte au *Parnasse*, où *Apollon* & les *Muses* sont placés en Cercle, & d'une maniére convenable; il ne manqueroit plus que d'entendre leurs doux Concerts, pour être véritablement enchanté du séjour qu'ils occupent ici. On a bien de la peine à quitter des Objets, & des *Points de vuë*, si agréables & si amusans! Mais on s'en console en entrant dans le charmant *Temple des Dames*. C'est un très bel *Edifice* de pierres de taille, dont le plain pié n'est qu'un *Portique* ouvert de tous cotés. L'Escalier très propre conduit à une *Salle* où tout ravit l'oeil; l'extrême propreté, la beauté des ornemens, & sur tout les belles peintures à l'huile dont tous les murs son décorés, [p.23] & qui représentent toutes sortes d'exercices convenables au *Beau Sexe*. Il semble que le *Peintre* se soit étudié à n'y peindre que des *Physionomies* séduisantes, & des *Minois* tout à fait aimables. Certes, *Mademoiselle*, je n'ai guéres rien vû de plus riant, ni de plus gracieux que cette belle *Salle*.

Un autre *Edifice* bien Majestueux se présente ensuite; c'est celui que l'on nomme le *Temple Impérial*. Il n'a qu'un seul *Salon* de plain-pié, où se trouvent les *Bustes* des *trois* meilleurs *Empéreurs* qui aient jamais règné, *Tite*, *Trajan*, & *Marc-Aurèle*. On voit sur la tête de l'un d'eux cette belle *maxime*, touchant le *Glaive* que portent les *Souverains*; qu'il *soit pour moi, si j'en suis digne, mais contre moi, si c'est le contraire!* En sortant de là, l'on arrive *au Temple de l'Amitié*. C'est un *Edifice* d'un goût tout différent, & très élégament orné. Il est rempli de *Bustes* illustres, mais je n'y ai vû celui d'aucun *Monarque*: Seroit ce pour insinuer que cette Espèce d'Hommes ne paroit pas être faite pour *aimer*, moins encore que pour *être aimée?* Quoi qu'il en soit, j'ai été charmé au moins d'y trouver un *Héritier-Présomptif de la Couronne*, Monseigneur le Prince de *Galles*, qui a des qualités excellentes, & qui [p.24] honore Mylord *Cobham* d'une *Amitié* particuliére. Je n'ai pas été moins agréablement flaté, d'y voir les *Bustes* de deux des plus beaux *Génies* que *l'Angleterre* ait aujourdhui, Mylord *Chesterfield*, & Mr. *George Littleton*, tous deux sensibles aux charmes de *l'Amitié*, à un point peu commun dans le siècle où nous vivons. Il y a de plus dans ce magnifique *Sallon* des Peintures très bien executées, telles que celle de *l'Amitié* au dessus de la Porte, celles de la *Justice*, & de la *Liberté*, &c. Il faut surtout remarquer le *Tableau* du *Plat-fonds*, qui est bien malin. C'est la *Brétagne* sous l'emblême d'une *Femme*, à qui l'on présente d'un coté *les deux Règnes qui lui ont aquis le plus de gloire*, sur des Cartons où on lit ces mots, *le Règne d'Elizabeth*, & *le Règne d'Edward* III, & de l'autre coté *le Règne qui lui a fait le plus de honte*, avec ces mots *le Règne de la Reine*, mais le *Nom* en est adroitement couvert de la main de la *Brétagne* qui le rejette; il n'est pas difficile sans doute de déviner quel *Règne* l'on a ici en vuë. Au reste, on admire beaucoup la *Statuë* du *Gladiateur*, qui est placée devant ce beau *Temple*; on prétend, qu'en l'envisageant de front elle paroit un *Chef-d'oeuvre*.

[p.25] J'oubliois presque de vous parler du beau *Pont* de pierres, nommé le *Pont-Palladien*, qui fait un si bel effet apperçu de tant de divers endroits de ce superbe *Jardin*. C'est un *Edifice* couvert & vouté, tout rempli de *bas-reliefs*, & de *Figures* très bien executées. On y voit les différentes *Parties du Monde* qui apportent leurs *productions* particuliéres à la *Brétagne*, & qui semblent lui en faire *hommage*. Il y a plusieurs de ces *Figures* qui ont une grande force.

Enfin, à quelque distance de ce *Pont* singulier, & assés proche de l'autre joli *Pont de bois*, s'éleve un *Edifice Gothique* très curieux & très sompteux. On ne sauroit imiter plus heureusement le *gôut ancien d'Architecture,* qu'on l'a fait dans cette occasion. C'est une espèce de *Chateau* à plusieurs étages, & qui domine presque sur tout le *Jardin.* La vuë en est admirable & tout à fait charmante. On ne se lasse point de contempler une si grande & si riante variété d'objets. C'est de là en particulier que l'on apperçoit sur *la droite,* un grand terrain, que Mylord *Cobham* destine à de nouveaux ornemens, & auxquels il fait travailler [p.26] à force. Comme je ne sais point son *Plan,* je ne saurois vous rien dire là dessus. Ce qu'il y a de bien certain, c'est qu'à en juger par les preuves qu'il a déja données de son *Gout* & de sa *Magnificence,* ces nouveaux embellissemens ne peuvent manquer d'être marqués au même coin. Mais pour revenir à nôtre *Chateau Gothique,* toutes les *vitres* en sont peintes à *l'antique,* & il y en a quelques unes qui sont d'une grande beauté. On ne voit en dedans pas le moindre ornement; & néanmoins on trouve du plaisir dans cette simplicité du tems *Jadis.* Tout *l'Edifice* paroit *vieux,* & il n'est pas même encore bien achevé. Il y a en cela beaucoup d'art. Au reste, on a êu soin de placer tout autour sur des *Piédestaux,* un grand nombre de *Bustes* qui représentent les *Divinités* des anciens *Saxons;* & ces *Bustes* paroissent extrémement *antiques,* quoi qu'ils soient tout à fait *modernes.*

Je ne vous parle point, *Mademoiselle,* de divers autres ornemens dont ce vaste *Jardin* est embelli; tels que le *Monument* du fameux *Congrève,* le *Tombeau* du Capitaine *Grenville,* neveu de Mylord *Cobham;* & plusieurs *Statues* remarquables. Il est impossible à un *Voïageur* [p.27] qui n'a guéres que 4 ou 5 heures pour parcourir tant de belles choses, de ne rien laisser échaper à sa curiosité, ou de se souvenir exactement de tout ce qu'il a vû; aussi me suis-je aidé pour me rappeller mes idées, des *Descriptions* imprimées en *Anglois* que l'on distribue à tous ceux qui se rendent à *Stow.* Je n'ajoute plus que cette seule Observation; c'est que pour rendre ce magnifique *Jardin* plus varié & plus parfait, on y a renfermé *la Ville,* pour ainsi dire & la *Campagne, l'Art* & la *Nature,* en y faisant entrer des *Prairies,* des *Champs,* des Troupeaux de *Brebis,* de *Daims,* & de *Chevreuils,* des *Monceaux de foin,* des *Villages,* & même des *Eglises;* car tout cela est compris dans son enceinte. D'ailleurs, ce qui contribuë extrémement a l'aggrandir, c'est qu'il n'est fermé d'aucune *haye* ni d'aucun *mur*, & que la *muraille* qui soutient la *Terrasse* en dehors, est à *rez de chaussée*; de sorte que rien absolument ne borne la vuë, & que cet immense *Jardin* semble se confondre avec toute la Campagne des environs, & s'y être pour ainsi dire enchassé, & incorporé. Assurément je ne crois pas qu'il y ait au monde une *Maison de Plaisance* aussi magnifique ni aussi charmante, dans toutes ses parties & ses Ornemens, [p.28] que l'est celle dont je viens de vous tracer un foible crayon. Vous n'y trouvez je l'avouë, ni *Jets-d'eau*, ni *Orangerie*, ni *Parterres*, ni *Symmétriques Colifichets*. Mais d'un coté, les *Anglois* ne peuvent souffrir l'ennuïeuse *régularité* des *Parterres*, ni ce nombre prodigieux de *fleurs* qui entêtent souvent & incommodent plus qu'elles ne plaisent; ils préfèrent à tout cela des *Tapis de Verdure*, & de *vastes Lits du plus beau gazon* qu'il y ait au Monde, avec de belles *allées d'Arbres*, de grandes *Piéces d'eau*, & des *vues étenduës* & *diversifiées* le plus qu'il est possible. D'un autre coté, Mylord *Cobham* dont le *Plan* n'est pas encore rempli, a peut être dessein d'y faire entrer des *Jets-d'eau*, qui sont sans contredit un des plus grands ornemens d'un *Jardin*, & qui acheveroient de mettre le comble à la beauté du sien. Ce n'est pas *l'eau* qui y manque, il y en a en abondance; & je doute que la *dépense* pût en arrêter l'entreprise, puisqu'elle est prodiguée dans tout le reste, & qu'elle y sent bien plus le *Souverain*, que le *Pair du Roïaume*.

Tel est *Mademoiselle* le séjour enchanté du fameux *Stow*, & cependant je ne vous ai rien [p.29] dit encore du Palais même de Mylord *Cobham*. C'est une charmante *Maison* presque toute *neuve*, & dont l'intérieur n'est pas entiérement achevé. *L'architecture* en est *Italienne*, & d'un goût très élégant. Le *Corps de logis* est grand, & décoré d'un rang de *Colonnes* dans le milieu du prémier Etage; il est soutenu de chaque coté de *deux Pavillons* un peu moins élevés, & sur le même front, & ceux-ci de *deux autres* plus petits encore, placés de même, & ornés de *Colonnes*; ce qui forme une façade superbe, & qui embrasse toute l'ouverture de la grande Allée. On monte à ce *Palais* par un *Perron* magnifique, & qui s'unit à une belle *Terrasse* qui règne le long de la *Maison*, & qui se termine par une douce rampe du coté du *Jardin.* Je ne m'arrêterai point à vous faire ici la description des *Appartemens,* ni des *Ameublemens* de ce riche *Palais.* Je me contente, *Mademoiselle,* de vous dire, que tout y est dans le *goût* moderne; *Sculpture dorée, Glaces* sans nombre, *Cadres* travaillés avec art, *Plat-fonds* bien peints, *Portrais* & *Tableaux* des meilleurs Maitres, *Bustes* de marbre, *Statuës, Cheminées* d'un grand goût, *Tables* précieuses, *Tapisseries* charmantes, *Meubles* dorés; en un mot, tout ce que l'on a imaginé jusques ici de plus riant & [p.30] de plus riche est comme prodigué dans ce beau *Palais.* Quel domage que le *Maitre* qui l'habite soit d'un âge si avancé; & qu'un Seigneur qui a le goût si exquis, & le coeur si grand & si généreux, ne puisse pas espérer de passer les bornes ordinaires de la vie humaine! De tels Exemples que le sien sont d'une grande utilité pour la Société; car sa *magnificence* contribue à faire subsister un très grand nombre de Personnes, qu'il emploie continuellement; & elle semble dire à tous les Grands qui sont dans *l'Opulence,* qu'elle n'est *honorable* que lorsqu'on sait en faire un usage *utile* à ses *Concitoïens.*

J'ai l'honeur d'être avec respect,

Londres ce $\frac{12}{23}$ de   Mademoiselle,
Septembre, 1748.

Votre très humble, &

très obéissant serviteur,

J. d. C.

F I N I S.

George Bickham (?1706 – 1771)

The Beauties of Stow (1750)

George Bickham the Younger came from a family of writing-masters and engravers, and was a typical publisher of Pope's generation, enterprising, versatile and unscrupulous. He entered the Stowe scene late in 1750, when he published an octavo guidebook entitled *The Beauties of Stow.* Like the bound collection of Seeley's guidebooks it cost five shillings.

Bickham's intention was to produce in a single volume the range of material which Seeley was offering in three, and to present it in a more attractive way, as if a well-informed guide were conducting a visitor round the gardens in person, commenting on the points of interest as they went. All the temples were clearly named and described, with the inscriptions and their translations printed in full, and nearby was an engraved picture, whole page or half page, to illustrate the building concerned. It was an astute piece of publishing, timed to exploit the uncertainty after Cobham's death, when Seeley had lost his patron, and it threatened to oust Seeley from the Stowe tourist market.

As evidence of Stowe's development, however, it is of little value. Analysis has shown that 98 per cent of its text has been lifted from sources already in print: 33 per cent from the *Description*, 36 per cent from the *Dialogue*, 18 per cent from *Les Charmes* and 11 per cent from Defoe's *Tour*. For only two per cent, less than forty lines out of sixty-seven pages, has no printed source been traced, and these contain almost nothing of importance.

Many of the illustrations, too, are copied from those previously published, but somewhat more confidence can be placed in them. It seems that Seeley's *Views* had been compared on the spot with the actual buildings before being redrawn, and a few of Bickham's illustrations were entirely new.

The real importance of *The Beauties of Stow* is that it provoked a battle of the guidebooks between Bickham and Seeley which continued for twelve years, both publishers trying to outdo the other by adding extra features to each new edition. In the end it was Seeley who won. After the appearance of his 1763 edition there was no reply from Bickham, who retired from the struggle. By that time Seeley's guidebook contained a well-documented tour of both house and gardens, illustrations of the garden front of the house and of the garden buildings, a plan of the gardens, a plan of the principal floor of the house, and measured drawings of twenty-one of the garden buildings. Everything an intelligent visitor could ask for was there. Yet the astonishing thing is that by that date no comprehensive guidebook had been published for any other country seat in England. The genre evolved and reached near perfection at Stowe in virtual isolation.

Several of Bickham's illustrations are reproduced in this volume, but the text is omitted. It can be found in *The Gardens at Stowe*, ed. J.D. Hunt, Vol. 16 in the series *The English Landscape Garden* (New York, 1982); and also in the edition published by the Augustan Reprint Society, ed. G.B. Clarke (Los Angeles, 1977), on the introduction to which this note is based.

Sophia, Lady Newdigate (1718 – 1774)

Sophia Conyers was married to Sir Roger-Newdigate of Arbury Hall in Warwickshire in 1743, and fortunately she shared his architectural and antiquarian enthusiasm. Parliamentary business regularly took him from Arbury to London, and they often made the journey together, taking the opportunity to stop on the way and visit houses where new building or alterations were in progress. They were at Stowe late in July 1748, probably on July 29th. Lady Newdigate wrote up their journal. The loose sheets of drawings which accompany it are in Sir Roger's hand and are likely to have been made on the same occasion.

By explicitly limiting her comments to what had been done within the previous two years, Lady Newdigate was probably implying that this was not her first visit, though she may have been relying on the guidebook, which she must surely have purchased, for details of earlier buildings. Her account is invaluable as a record of precisely which buildings had just been completed and which were under construction at the date of her visit, and also for the otherwise unknown details of the Verona-style "amphitheatre" which was projected in the Grecian Valley. One would like to know which member of the Stowe staff the Newdigates got all this information from. And did they always take a tape measure or rule with them on their travels, so that they could measure the details of a building, like the Chinese House, correct to the nearest inch?

from her *Journal* (1748)

The Country hereabouts is very unpleasant, but began to Improve within two miles of Buckingham. Very near the town lies Finmore the seat of Mr. Poulett. The house is situated in the middle of a small park very full of Timber which comes up close to the Great Road. From hence we had a fine view of Stowe the seat of Lord Cobham to which we were prevented going that evening by rain. Buckingham where we passd the night is a large Town tolerably well built but has nothing remarkable enough to detain us. In the morning early we set out for Stowe two miles off. This place is so well known that it is unecessary as well as impossible to describe it. I shall only mention those things that are new within these two years. The house is much enlarged being now one of the longest fronts in England, but it ought to be observed that several offices lye in the line of building in order to make it so. There are two Noble Apartments newly built, a Ball room 70 feet by 25 and 25 high richly furnished the pictures extreamly bad, beyond that is a drawing room furnished with Crimson velvet and hung with whole lengths of all the Grenville family, and further on is a large bedchamber and dressing room fitted up very elegantly with Chints Chinese pictures and Indian Cabinets and opens into a Loggia which makes the Apartment extreamly agreable. These rooms with the Chappel, which is handsomely fitted up and has a mosaick cieling of white and gold, is the additional building on one side. On the other is a Gallery 75 feet by 25 and 20 high, a drawing room 30 by 25, and a prodigious large bedchamber of which I could not learn the dimensions, in which the bed is to be raisd upon steps and is intended, as the person who shewd the house told us, for any of the Royal Family, if ever they should do my Lord the honour of a visit. This apartment is to be fitted up with the greatest Magnificence, it is at present only brick walls yet said to have cost ten thousand pounds. The Gardens are daily adding to. The Gothick Church is now compleat, in which Uniformity of Taste is more apparent than in any other building among the numbers here, the windows are painted Glass some of which is extreamly fine. The Ladies Temple is also finished, with which I cannot say we were much delighted. In the view of it is lately erected a naval pillar in honour of Captain Grenville, on the Top stands a figure of Neptune with a splinter of the ship in his hands, and on the base of the pillar is inscribed great encomiums on this unfortunate young man. There are several grand designs on foot as a model of an ancient amphitheatre at Verona which is to be about 500 feet in circumference, the Arena of its Original is about that dimension. Near this they are copying the maison Quarré at Nismes a prodigious building of which the foundation only is laid. Lady Cobham is building a model of the Trajan Pillar to the honour of her Lord, on the Top of which is to stand a statue of him. Every year makes great additions to the size of these gardens and to the crowd of buildings. The latter ones are in a much better taste than the former but if they were thinner sown would be much more pleasing to the eye. After walking between five and six miles we were heartily glad to get into the Coach where we refresh'd ourselves with a pot of Coffee and went back through Buckingham.

(Warwick CRO, CR 1841/7, ff. 3-5)

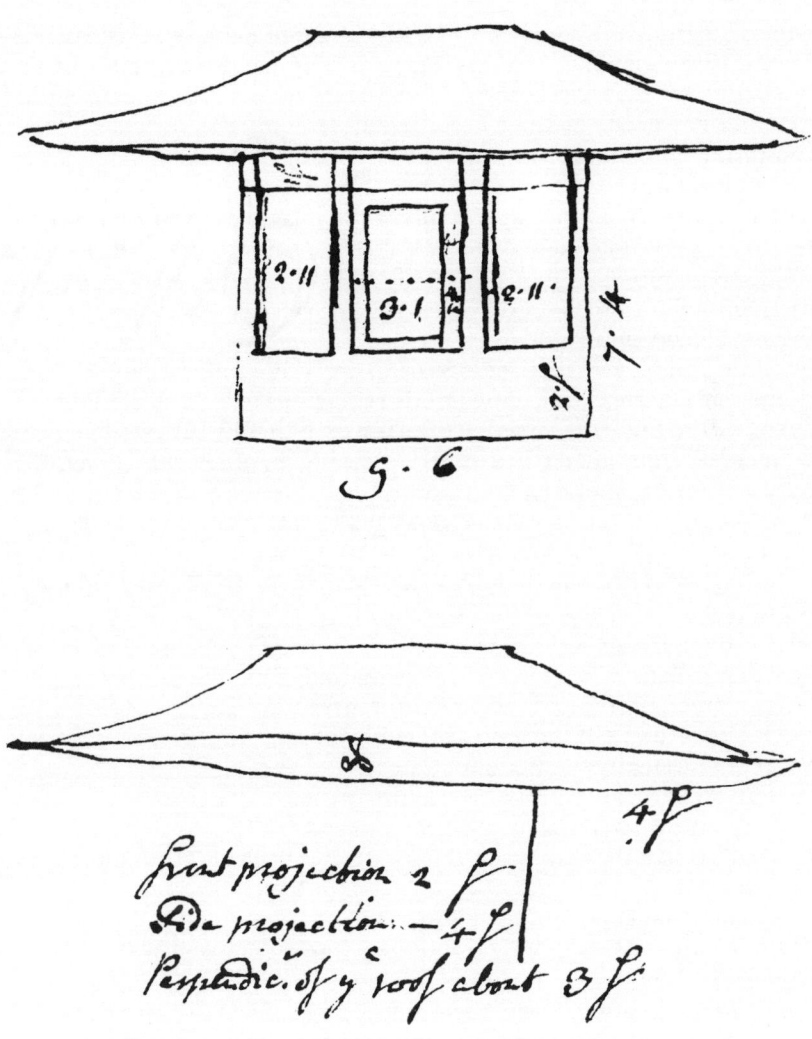

Sketch of the Chinese House by Sir Roger Newdigate
from Lady Newdigate's *Journal* (enlarged)

Jemima, Marchioness Grey (1722 – 1797)

Granddaughter and sole heir of Henry, Duke of Kent, of Wrest Park in Bedfordshire, Jemima, Marchioness Grey, was married to Philip Yorke, later the 2nd Earl of Hardwicke, of Wimpole in 1740, thus bringing together two of the greatest East Anglian families. She travelled widely round England, and this outspoken comment on Stowe is taken from her letterbook.

The opinions put into the mouth of the imaginary visitor Polython by Gilpin were not the only adverse criticisms directed at the artificial character of Stowe's gardens. As early as 1738, after a journey through the mountainous scenery of Wales, Bishop Herring had written to his friend William Duncombe:

> "I am afraid, if I had seen Stow in my way home, I should have thrown out some very unmannerly reflections upon it; I should have smiled at the little niceties of art, and beheld with contempt an artificial ruin, after I had been agreeably terrified with something like the rubbish of a creation."

A few years later, in his blank verse poem *The Enthusiast*, which was subtitled *The Lover of Nature* (1744), Joseph Warton asked the more radical question of whether a garden like Stowe could ever compete with the natural beauty of the countryside:

> "Lead me from Gardens deckt with Art's vain Pomps.
> Can gilt alcoves, can marble-mimic gods,
> Parterres embroider'd, obelisks, and urns
> Of high relief; can the long, spreading lake,
> Or vista lessening to the sight; Can Stow
> With all her Attic fanes, such raptures raise,
> As the thrush-haunted copse…?"

Reflections like these indicate the groundswell which was building up against what was later described, by George Lyttelton, as "the stiffness of the old Bridgeman Taste" at Stowe.

But neither the poet nor the bishop has the impact of this young woman in her mid-twenties, who wrote down her thoughts after walking round Stowe at the beginning of July 1748. She knew she was taking a heretical view, but hers was the authentic voice of the next generation. She stripped the garden of its pretensions like the child in the story of the Emperor's new clothes.

from the *Letterbook of Jemima, Marchioness Grey* (1748)

Wrest, July 5th 1748.

— I seem to have owed you a Letter a long while, ever since my Expedition to Stowe which I fancy you must have wanted an Account of, and I have not yet found an Opportunity to send it you. —My Opinion of Stowe will read I fancy very Paradoxicaly, for I think it a Place as well worth passing a few Hours in, and yet what I would least chuse to live at of any I ever saw: and that both exceeded my Expectation and disappointed it. Stowe is more extensive, seems more vast and magnificent than I had imagined, the Garden they say contains Three hundred Acres, and there is something more advantageous and great in its Situation being up the Side of a Hill than I suppos'd. But then for such an Extent (which is quite a Country), there is the least of Management or Beauty in the Disposing of it, it affords the least Variety and Surprise, and fewer pleasant Spots that would suit your Ideas of the Country or a Garden than you can imagine. Nature has done very little for it, and Art so much that you cannot possibly be deceiv'd, but whichever way you turn you see vast Expence and Labor and the Whole to be a stiff set Plan; so much so that could I Draw I might send you from Memory a pretty exact Sketch of the Garden. There is scarcely anything concealed in it, or any Object you come upon without having seen it a Mile off and in fifty different Views in your Journey of Five Miles round the Enclosure. Indeed it is of a Size to bear this, and the Objection is not the same in so vast a Scheme as when you overlook at Once the whole of a small Design. Perhaps too as the only Aim of the Place is Shew, it may answer that End, but still it greatly lessens the real Beauty and Contrivance in it.

The Garden is at the Bottom and round the Brow of a Hill: the Account of its Size is no less Shewy than the rest, since the Side of this Hill is for the greater part taken up with two ugly rough Fields; and the general Plan of it is thus, —in the lower Part there is first a Gravel Terrass, then some Pieces of Water of different Shapes, and that make in all between Twenty and Thirty Acres of Water about which there is some Wood, and in the middle part of the Garden nearest the House (which stands at the top of the Hill) are some inclosed shady Places pretty enough, the rest is all open and bare. —The two green Fields rise from the Water up the Sides of the Hill (one on each hand right and left of the House) and the Gravel Terrass goes round them along the Brow, interspersed or rather filled with Buildings, parted from the Field by a Sunk Fence, and just enough Wood behind it to stop your View and keep you from the Boundary. There is the Appearance of a few Winding Walks there, but dark and damp without a Twig of Underwood, though being under the Shade of a few high Trees (a Rarity at Stow) whose Branches afforded Roost to a parcel of Bantams and Turkeys, they were tolerably pleasant.

That Side of the Garden first finish'd is so Crowded with Buildings that as you see them at a distance seem almost at Top of One Another that each loses its Effect. They are all small and trifling or clumsy, and are all dirty and decaying already. For the Owner I am convinced has neither much Taste or Genius in the forming his Works or any Notion of Enjoyment from them afterwards. The Vanity of making what shall be seen and talked of by Strangers carries him on to new Enlargements and Buildings from Year to Year, while those that are done are neglected, and he just affords some Hours of a Sunday being a long idle Day to go round his Garden. Indeed it is only fit for a Public One, there is scarcely any Shade or Retirement to be found in it: You are seen from One End of it to the Other, and there is always Company of various sorts to see you. In short the general Character of the Place is Vast and Magnificent, but Elegant and Comfortable are two Words the most opposite to it that is possible. You may guess in what Manner its Appearance struck me, when I tell you that at our Return Wrest even to my Eyes look'd as a Model only, a Garden in Miniature: —but on the Other hand One that I would not change not even for a Week upon any Condition.

That Side of the Garden at Stowe latest done has not such a Number of Buildings: (such a Grove of them as One has justly

heard it call'd, they tell you there are in all 33) and they are
reckon'd better but even these are very heavy. The Temple to
Friendship is reckoned the Best, but that to Female Friendship
is the best Room, indeed the Only good One, for everything
(as I said before) is Outside, and in all these Buildings there is
hardly a Room you would chuse to set down in, or excepting
these Two that would hold half a Dozen People. The Gothic
Building half Church half Tower in Appearance, is the most
Uncommon and best in its Way. It stands very high and expos'd,
but in return makes a good Point of View, and has the finest
Prospect over the Garden and Country of any. It is built of
Reddish Stone, and the Windows are filled with Painted Glass,
it looks quite over the Garden, with the most inclos'd woody
Part of it lying underneath with Buildings rising among the
Trees, and over them the House which has now the longest
Front (they tell you) in England, and being Whited Over has
a very good Effect, and is a fine Object to several Places below
it. There has been large Wings added to it of late, that have
made it of this Size and that have large Rooms in them, and it
seems a handsome good House within Doors.

Before it is the Oldest Part of the Garden and said to be the
Worst; a green Parterre with Evergreens and a Hedge round
it, and a Narrow Walk of high Trees down the Hill. I think I
lik'd it better than most people do, because it seem'd Private
(and indeed the only thing well contriv'd there, is that what
Shade the Place affords is in the Part nearest the House), but
it certainly is not an Opening anserable to the rest.

Amongst the inclos'd Spots, the prettiest is what they call the
Elysian Fields which is a Winding Canal with green Banks and
scatter'd Trees upon them. A Wall of Niches filled with Busts
of antient Worthies is by the Canal and at One End rais'd a
little above it is the Temple of Antient Virtue; Small and I think
heavy, but One of the better sort amongst the Buildings.
Another, is the Grotto at the end of a small Piece of Serpentine
Water like the Other with Green all round it, and the Shellwork
is pretty. There is also a Chinese Room the prettiest I have seen,
and the Only One like the Drawings and Prints of their Houses.
It stands in a little dirty Piece of Water with Steps like a Bridge

to the Shore, and a Gallery and Rail round the room which you may suppose is very small. It has four Latticed Windows, the Wall and the Roof painted in the Chinese manner and the Inside quite wainscotted with Japan: a great many Old Screens have been cut to pieces (I fancy) to make it, but it is Fine and Pretty.

All that remains particularly to be mention'd is your first Entrance into the Garden which has nothing very great and striking in it (and that too is into the middle and oldest Part). You rise out of a Sunk Fence through an Iron Pallisade upon the Middle of the Outward Gravel Terrass in the Lower Part of the Garden, with a little open Pavilion on each Side of the Gate. Before you is a Bason of Water, an Obelisk in it, and that narrow steep Walk that leads up to the Parterre and the House: you have a Side View on each Hand up the Hill, and see several Buildings at a great distance. —By the by, those same Fields up the Sides of the Hill are exceeding ugly things. I suppose their Roughness and Unevenness is design'd as a Contrast to the great Regularity and Ornament of the Objects that surround them. But it is hard upon poor Nature and playing Booty with her to take her Defects and not her Beauties; and that the only thing remaining in the State she left it should be a bare rough Hill, when a little Help (and not Disguise) might have smooth'd it into a level green Lawn with a few Clumps or single Trees scattered over it, and made it by far the most beautiful Object there. What a strange Want of Judgment does it seem not to have hit upon this! But my Lord is too great a Friend to Art to trust Nature in her best Dress, knowing how much the first would lose in the Comparison and her simple Beauties get the better of all his Vain Pomp.

Now to describe the rest of the Water, —on the Left of the Bason there is a Lake of Nine or Ten Acres which is handsome; at the End is a Piece of Rockwork that turns into a Cascade when you bid it, and by it a bad-dish Sort of Hermitage; on the opposite Bank this Field rises, and there are Temples over one-another's Heads without End. To the Right Hand the Water is form'd into a Serpentine River that afterwards divides, and in all contains about Eight or Ten Acres more, one narrow Branch turns among the Trees and so on (I believe) to the

Elysian Fields, Grotto etc. but its End is well conceal'd, and the Other runs and is stop'd by a Palladian Bridge, the same as at Wilton, only that here the farthest Side from you is filled up with a monstrous-siz'd Bas-relief, of the History of Commerce and the Four Quarters of the World bringing their Productions to Britannia.

Besides all here mention'd, there are now going on Improvements in the 60 Acres last inclos'd, which is a Fall and Rise again of the Hill on the Opposite Side behind that which is already finished. But even this by the Laying-out seems to have no sort of Variety. The Slopes bare like the Other Side with Walks up or round them; a Piece of Water is to be in the Valley below, and vast Buildings larger and mightier than all the Others upon the Sides: —Sure this is not Taste or Judgment!

The Park surrounds the Garden, and that part nearest it is bare like itself and not pleasant: but at a distance and Out of Sight are fine Woods with Ridings through them. The Country about it is a high Flat, dirty and not at all beautiful. —And here I have tired myself and my Pen with Stowe as I did my Legs with Walking Over it. —We got to an Inn just by it to Dinner, were about four Hours in the Garden (and had not Feet or Spirits to walk through every part of it neither) or in the House where (there being no Family) we got some Tea and return'd to lye at the same Inn. —

But if you are not tired with Reading you shall have the rest of our Expedition another Time.

We went from Stowe the next Morning to Lord Pomfret's, through fine Woods and a Country prettily inclos'd but very dirty and bad.

(Bedfordshire RO, L30/9a/1, ff. 164 - 75)

Anne Grenville, afterwards Countess Temple
(?1708 – 1777)

Anne Grenville wrote this letter from London to her husband Richard, later Earl Temple, who was in Buckinghamshire, either at Stowe or Wotton. The date is not given but must have been 1750. For Richard Grenville inherited Stowe on the death of his uncle, Lord Cobham, in September 1749, and the letter was clearly written after the widowed Lady Cobham had moved out of Stowe and before 'Capability' Brown, nominally head gardener but effectively steward, handed over his responsibilities in November 1750. (Strictly, in the year 1750 Richard Grenville was himself Lord Cobham, a courtesy title which was his for a couple of years, but to call him that here might cause misunderstanding.)

It can never be easy to take over a great house like Stowe on the death of its previous owner without causing offence to the surviving widow, especially when the heir is a nephew rather than a son. On this occasion it was made even more difficult by the cool relations which had existed for several years between the Grenvilles of Wotton and the Cobhams of Stowe. In his old age Lord Cobham was no longer quite the affable host and uncle he had been earlier, and Lady Cobham had become extremely difficult. "La signora est arrivée avec son epoux," J. de Pesters wrote to Lady Denbigh in 1745. "Elle m'a paru plus maussade, plus grondeuse et plus absurde que jamais." And in the following year Anne Grenville described arriving at Stowe as entering "the house of Discord". No doubt the family friction recorded in her letter was made worse by the problems of taking over Stowe, but it was nothing new.

The letter also establishes that from the start Earl Temple had a mind of his own, and, since he was the nephew of Cobham, he was freed from any inhibitions a son might have had about altering things which his father had carried out. When he moved from Wotton to Stowe, he took with him his steward, his head gardener and a wooden barn, which was dismantled and re-erected in the park. Brown departed at the end of the estate year to set up as a consultant on his own, a parting which seems to have been entirely amicable. His wife stayed on at Stowe through the winter until their next child was born, Brown himself was lent £100, and a few years later he was commissioned to carry through an extensive landscaping scheme at Wotton. But he did no more work at Stowe, and from the moment of his departure Earl Temple was his own master-gardener. He immediately took the reins of management into his own hands, as this letter shows, though it was a little time before he gained the confidence to design major landscaping projects himself. Though he would probably not have admitted it, his subsequent alterations indicate that he shared many of the critical views of the Marchioness Grey. In time he transformed the Stowe he had inherited into the idealised landscape we know today.

from a *Letter to Richard Grenville, afterwards Earl Temple (1750)*

Saturday

My dearest,

I went to Court yesterday and was very well receiv'd by the King. He asked if the Gardens at Stow were big enough or whether all the estate was to be put into gardens, but mighty good humour'd, laugh'd a good deal and I believe meant a little sneer at the last owner of them. I went to my Lady Cobham yesterday and she began in a violent manner about the Sheep being put into the garden. I told her they look'd mighty pretty and that everybody said it wou'd make the turf much firmer, but if they did harm they woud be taken out I suppos'd, but that I really never disputed any thing with you for I thought you knew much better than I, and she said she shou'd scold you well when she saw you. I knew what I was to meet with for she told Brown she had cry'd all night and never slept a wink about it and raved [and tore] and said if my Lord Cobham cou'd know how Stow was used how vext he woud be, and he said Lady Temple and Lady Hester were in an uproar about it too. They were both by when she begun with me but they button'd up their mouths and said not one word. Now one shou'd imagine they might have try'd to stop her instead of setting her to work, considering you are a party concern'd. I wish you wou'd ask Brown what she said to him for I have not seen him, but she has begun with Farrand in hopes… It happened at a bad time for me for I was very ill and low spirited yesterday and she worried me almost to death. I fancy you will be tired enough with her and the less we see her and have to do with her the better.

(BL Add. MS 57806, f. 76)

Epilogue

Evidence of impending change comes from a distinguished foreign visitor, Stanislas-Auguste Poniatowski, later elected King of Poland. In 1754 he visited Stowe, where he met Earl Temple and his Grenville brothers and was guided round the gardens by Earl Temple himself. The enthusiasm he found for the new style of gardening made him reflect that the attitude of Englishmen on this subject was almost fanatical.

"Ce nouveau goût, qui consiste principalement à produire des paysages artificiels dans les lieux qu'on veut décorer, était devenu une espèce de secte nouvelle et en avait presque toute la ferveur et toute l'antipathie intolérante contre la doctrine ancienne. Je ne me hasardai qu'une fois ou deux de témoigner quelque regret sur l'exclusion totale de tout alignement, en fait d'eaux ou d'allées. Je vis que je risquais de déchoir de la faveur assez générale que me procurait l'amitié de Charles Yorke, mon introducteur, et la disposition sincère où j'étais à révérer et à aimer les Anglais et presque tous leurs goûts et leur manière d'être…"

(Mémoires du roi Stanislas-Auguste Poniatowski, St. Petersburg, 1914, Vol.I, p.120)